THEMES
for early years

SUMMER

SU GARNETT

THEMES
for early years

Author Su Garnett
Editor Jane Bishop
Assistant editors Lesley Sudlow/Susan Howard
Series designer Lynne Joesbury
Designer Rachael Hammond
Illustrations Louise Gardner
Cover Lynne Joesbury
Action Rhymes, Poems and Stories compiled by Jackie Andrews
Songs compiled by Peter Morrell
Assemblies chapter by Lesley Prior

Designed using Adobe Pagemaker
Processed by Scholastic Ltd, Leamington Spa

Published by Scholastic Ltd, Villiers House, Clarendon Avenue, Leamington Spa, Warwickshire CV32 5PR
© 1999 Scholastic Ltd Text © 1999 Su Garnett
1 2 3 4 5 6 7 8 9 9 0 1 2 3 4 5 6 7 8

The publishers gratefully acknowledge permission to reproduce the following copyright material:
Tony Bradman for 'Sticky licky' from *Smile Please* © 1987, Tony Bradman, (1987, Puffin); **Ann Bryant** for 'Summer street party' © 1999, Ann Bryant, previously unpublished; **Sue Cowling** for 'Ready for the beach' © 1999, Sue Cowling, previously unpublished; **Elizabeth Dale** for 'Sunshine and shadows' © 1999, Elizabeth Dale, previously unpublished; **Sue Croft** for 'Strawberry and Cream' © 1999, Sue Croft, previously unpublished; **Susan Eames** for 'Pack my suitcase' © 1999, Susan Eames, previously unpublished; **Val Jeans-Jakobsson** for 'Summer senses' © 1999, Val Jeans-Jakobsson, previously unpublished; **Penny Kent** for 'Our school fête' © 1999, Penny Kent, previously unpublished; **Karen King** for 'Harry's seaside holiday' © 1999, Karen King, previously unpublished; **Wendy Larmont** for 'Summer storm', 'Cover up' and 'Carnival' © 1999, Wendy Larmont, previously unpublished; **Johanne Levy** for 'Playing out' © 1999, Johanne Levy, previously unpublished; **Vikki MacRae** for 'In the heat' © 1999, Vikki MacRae, previously unpublished; **Trevor Millum** for words to 'In the heat' © 1999, Trevor Millum, previously unpublished; **Tony Mitton** for 'Seaside song' from *Finger Rhymes*, compiled by **John Foster** © 1996, Tony Mitton (1996, OUP); **Barbara Moore** for 'By the sea' and 'In the sky' © 1999, Barbara Moore, previously unpublished; Thomas Nelson and Sons Ltd for 'Mr Rabbit and the moon' from *New Way: Two Folk Tales* © 1993, Thomas Nelson and Sons Ltd; **Judith Nicholls** for 'What am I?' and 'Riddle-me-ree' © 1999, Judith Nicholls, previously unpublished and 'Strawberry pie' from *Jigglewords* by Judith Nicholls © 1993, Judith Nicholls (1993, Nelson); **Sue Nicholls** for 'Pot-pourri' © 1999, Sue Nicholls, previously unpublished; **Gill Parker** for the music to 'Sun and sand' © 1999, Gill Parker, previously unpublished; **Jan Pollard** for 'Summer skies' © 1999, Jan Pollard, previously unpublished; **Lesley Prior** for three assemblies © 1999, Lesley Prior, previously unpublished; **Stevie Ann Wilde** for 'Watch the wheat grow' and 'A letter to the grown-ups' © 1999, Stevie Ann Wilde, previously unpublished; **Brenda Williams** for 'Disappearing puddles' and 'Five wobbly jelly fish' © 1999, Brenda Williams, previously unpublished.
Every effort has been made to trace copyright holders and the publishers apologise for any inadvertent omissions.

British Library Cataloguing-in-Publication Data A catalogue record for this book is available from the British Library.

ISBN 0-590-53863-2

THEMES
for early years

CONTENTS

ACTIVITIES

INTRODUCTION

Of all the seasons of the year, summer is perhaps the one we all look forward to the most!

How can we use the children's natural enthusiasm for this topic to help them learn? Firstly, by providing stimulating and exciting learning experiences within a topic which is already of interest to them. Secondly, by introducing aspects of that topic in an integrated way which encourages as much active participation from them as possible. Delivering curriculum subjects in this integrated way prevents the learning process from becoming disjointed and maintains spontaneity in your group, allowing the freedom to explore children's suggested links to their own previous learning.

This book provides ideas for exciting activities which will fulfil the requirements of the Desirable Outcomes for Children's Learning for children in the three-to-six age range, while preparing for the National Curriculum and Scottish 5–14 Guidelines.

Young children are naturally very inquisitive and need time to explore their theories. An integrated topic approach allows them to do this, without losing any of the learning in different curriculum areas. The choice of topic is obviously very important; it must be one that children can relate to through their own experiences, thus making it easy to extend their initial learning and understanding. The topic of 'Summer' fulfils these needs and is an ideal one to choose!

USING THE SUMMER THEME

Most of us welcome the arrival of summer. It is a time we associate with long, sunny days, warm, light evenings, holidays and having fun. We start to think about 'the great outdoors' and we benefit from extra activity and plenty of exposure to fresh air.

It is important for children to make the most of this happy time and by building on their natural enthusiasm for being outside, we can share with them some of the interesting and beautiful things to be seen at this time of year. All children will be able to identify some ways in which the summer directly affects them – the clothes they wear, the food they eat and holidays they have.

Each chapter in the book looks at a different aspect of summer.

Chapter 1 (Signs of summer) focuses on careful observation of various natural phenomena such as shadows, evaporation and reflections and includes

a look at thunderstorms, hot-air balloons and minibeasts.

Chapter 2 (The sun) looks at the sun's effect in different areas of the world, its central importance to the universe and mankind and the light and heat it produces. The activities enable children to think about the need to protect themselves from the sun's rays, grow sunflower seeds and provide opportunities to explore melting.

Chapter 3 (Outdoor activities) concentrates on the countryside and playing fields and parks. The senses are used as children imagine themselves engaged in outdoor activities such as bicycling, summer fêtes and sports days that are the focus of this chapter.

In Chapter 4 (Summer food) the children have opportunities to handle summer food and take part in a discussion about likes and dislikes. The activities encourage children to think about where summer food comes from and how it is preserved; and how it was in the past.

Chapter 5 (Summer clothes) takes a look at the design of clothes intended to be worn in hot weather and for various summer sports. Clothes worn in other cultures are looked at including the materials used, colours and shapes.

The last activity chapter, Chapter 6 (Holidays), includes a look at seaside holidays, considers why people need holidays and talks about the necessary preparation for them. Activities include looking at different types of holidays, the different locations people choose and the luggage that they need to take with them. Early travel is also discussed.

HOW TO USE THIS BOOK

This book has been designed to provide adults working in the Early Years with all the necessary practical ideas and resources to work through a complete topic based on the theme of 'Summer'. The topic is subdivided into several smaller topics for ease of reference and also to allow for a very flexible approach to the suggested work. You may, for instance, find that your own group is particularly interested in 'the sun' aspect of summer so you may choose to use this chapter as your starting point or find this is where you will want to spend the most time. How long you wish to continue with each sub-topic will obviously depend on individual circumstances.

The book provides a very varied and flexible teaching resource and the sub-topics and activities can be used in any way or order that is desired.

TOPIC WEB

The Topic Web on pages 8 and 9 shows how all the activities relate to both the National Curriculum and the Scottish 5–14 Guidelines. To provide children with a balanced curriculum, the Topic Web shows an even distribution of activities between curriculum subjects, although some overlap will occur. You may photocopy these pages to help you plan your theme.

ACTIVITY PAGES

Each chapter in this section relates to a different aspect of the summer theme. Each activity has a primary focus on one area of the curriculum although, as an integrated topic approach is being

used, other areas of learning often arise. For example, when learning about maps (geography), children will also be involved in a lot of speaking and listening (English). All the activities contain a practical element, many involving close co-operation between members of the group, so encouraging development of language and social skills.

The activities are all arranged in the same way starting with the 'Objective' which identifies the main curriculum area and gives a concise statement about what the children are expected to learn from participating in the activity. A suggestion is then given for the appropriate group size, but obviously individual circumstances, for example the availability of adult support, may well influence your choice. However, general discussions and explanations can usually be held with and given to the whole group. It may then be necessary to split the group into smaller numbers in order to complete the practical part of the activities.

A list of materials, resources and equipment required to complete the activity is given under 'What you need'. Any books mentioned in the text will also be listed with other recommended materials on page 96.

The 'Preparation' section highlights the things that you, or you and the children, will need to do before you start the main activity. Proper preparation will help speed up the actual activity and ensure that all children can be immediately involved in the task.

'What to do' explains how to achieve the objective set out at the beginning of the activity. Suggestions are given for setting the 'scene' in order to capture the children's interest and imagination, before they become actively involved in the practical part of the activity. Precise instructions are given, but it is important to be flexible in your approach so that children can explore their own ideas and suggestions. For most activities, children are encouraged to work as independently as possible, with the minimum of adult help, so that they will feel a real sense of achievement having completed the task. However, you may feel you need to intervene in order to offer help on occasions, depending on the ability of the children in your group.

The 'Discussion' section is designed to extend the children's previous learning, developing their interest through open-ended questioning and

ASSEMBLIES

This chapter offers ideas for simple assemblies involving all the children, based on the theme of 'Summer'. There are also suggestions for reflections after the assembly, songs and prayers.

RESOURCES

This section is photocopiable. It provides a selection of action rhymes and poems, stories and songs linked to the theme. These resources have been chosen to supplement the theme of 'Summer' and much of the material has been specially commissioned. The resources are referred to in the main activities and follow-up suggestions wherever appropriate but can also be used as and when desired as stand-alone activity sheets.

PHOTOCOPIABLE SHEETS

These photocopiable sheets are designed to reinforce some of the main activities in the book and have been carefully chosen to provide work in a variety of curriculum areas. It is important to explain to the children exactly how they should use each sheet and to make sure that they all understand before they begin.

RECOMMENDED MATERIALS

The final page of the book provides a list of story books, information books, teachers' books, poetry, art and music that you may find useful for your 'Summer' theme.

testing their understanding of what they have been doing. It will sometimes be appropriate to ask questions during the activity and sometimes after it has been completed. Again, it is important for children to pursue their own thoughts and theories, so make sure you allow time for this.

In 'Follow-up activities', suggestions are given to reinforce the learning that has come from the activity itself and to extend that understanding and knowledge. Many of the ideas will also encourage interest and learning in other areas of the curriculum.

DISPLAYS

Displays add greatly to the children's enjoyment, understanding and learning of a topic. They are an important part of every Early Years setting and should be made as bright and attractive as possible so that they provide a constant talking point.

This chapter provides ideas for several specific displays linked to the theme of summer in general and to some of the activities in particular. Each display has been made as interactive as possible and includes suggestions for items that the children can touch and examine. Children should be encouraged to bring in items from home to add to displays and those who can read should be encouraged to read the signs to their peers. It is important that all the children know what the various labels on the display say.

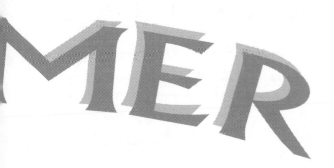

ENVIRONMENTAL STUDIES

PREPARING FOR PRIMARY SCHOOL

THE NATIONAL CURRICULUM

The National Curriculum for England and Wales specifies those areas and aspects of the curriculum which should be taught to children in state schools between the ages of five and sixteen. It is not compulsory for children in pre-school education or in independent schools, although many educators in these sectors select material for their teaching programmes from within the National Curriculum.

The 'core' subjects in the National Curriculum are English, Mathematics and Science, with History, Geography, Design and Technology, Information Technology, Art, Music, Physical Education and Religious Education making up the remainder.

The National Curriculum provides a Programme of Study for each subject and asks teachers to assess the level of attainment of each child in the country when they reach Year Two (age six to seven), partly by the use of nationwide tests, but mostly by asking teachers to use their professional judgement to allocate an overall level to each child.

Children need to develop vital learning skills before they are ready for the more formal National Curriculum. These include improving concentration, communication skills, social skills, hand / eye co-ordination and careful use of all their senses as detailed in the QCA's *Desirable Outcomes for children's learning on entering compulsory education*. Most nurseries and playgroups will find that the experiences they are offering children will be laying a good foundation for their future learning in school.

The activities in this book are designed to prepare children for the National Curriculum by developing these important skills. Children will be provided with a firm foundation on which to build their future learning. The theme approach helps children to learn in all the different curriculum areas in a way which is specifically geared towards their interest, rather than being strictly subject based. Each activity in the book is focused on a particular learning objective. The children's personal and social development is an ongoing theme that is incorporated throughout the activities in this book. The Topic web on pages 8 and 9 shows how each activity relates to a different subject area.

THE SCOTTISH 5–14 NATIONAL GUIDELINES

In Scotland there are national guidelines for schools on what should be taught to children between the ages of five and fourteen. These National Guidelines are divided into six main curriculum areas: English Language, Mathematics, Environmental Studies, Expressive Arts, Religious and Moral Education and Personal and Social Development.

Within these main areas, further subjects are found, for example, 'Expressive arts' includes Art and Design, Drama, Music and PE. Strands are also identified within each subject, for example Mathematics includes problem-solving and enquiry, and shape, position and movement.

CHAPTER 1
SIGNS OF SUMMER

Clear cloud patterns in the sky, beautiful reflections, insect activity, shadows and thunderstorms are all signs that summer is here. Show the children how to spot these signs and enjoy summer with these activities.

HIGH IN THE SKY

Objective

Art – To create a summer sky picture using a variety of art techniques.

Group size

Eight children.

What you need

White poster paint, brushes, sponge brushes, pieces of natural sponge, a roll and balls of cotton wool, PVA glue, bright blue card or sugar paper, white chalk, thin metal comb, pictures showing different cloud formations (use postcards, magazines and reference books) in the sky.

Preparation

Spread out your collection of coloured pictures or photographs of summer skies so that all the group can see. Lay out the art materials ready for use.

What to do

Carefully examine the pictures or photographs together. Look for different cloud formations and then encourage the children to think of ideas for reproducing these using various art techniques and the available collage materials.

High, thin cloud could be made using small pieces of cotton wool teased out very thinly from the roll. Large, white 'cauliflower' clouds can be represented by cotton wool balls piled on top of each other. Windy, 'mare's tails' can be drawn by turning chalk on its side or by combing thick poster paint. 'Mackerel back' sky can be very effectively transferred to blue card by printing with pieces of natural sponge dipped into rather

dry white paint. It should be possible to reproduce all other cloud shapes and patterns by using brushes and sponge paintbrushes of different thicknesses.

Encourage the children to experiment and try out their own ideas to produce a selection of cloud pictures. Display the finished results around your room on deep blue backing paper or as a backdrop for a 'summer' display.

Discussion

Talk about how we can tell what the weather is going to be like from the formation of the clouds in the sky. What does the sky look like when it is about to rain? When the weather is fine, what colours are the sky and any clouds? Do the clouds move across the sky faster when it is windy? What happens to the shape of them?

Follow-up activities

✧ Reproduce a stormy sky with black thunder clouds, rain and streaks of lightning.
✧ Keep a cloud chart for a week, drawing the cloud formations for each day. Relate this to the general weather pattern in your discussions.
✧ Look for line patterns in the sky which are not clouds (aeroplane trails). Can the children guess what has caused these?
✧ Try to observe birds flying in large formations. Watch for the specific shape of the flock.
✧ Sing the song 'In the sky' on page 84 and say together the poem 'Summer skies' on page 67.

NOW YOU SEE IT...

Objective

Science – To look at the process of evaporation.

Group size

Whole group.

What you need

Water, a washing-up bowl, several small pieces of clothing in different types of material, clothes pegs, a clothes line, a doll with long hair, a towel and a hairdryer, a sunny, preferably windy day.

Preparation

Half fill the washing-up bowl with warm soapy water. Set up the clothes line outside within easy reach of the children.

What to do

Explain that you will all be doing some washing together and that afterwards you will wash the doll's hair in order to find out how wet things get dry again. Do we have to dry everything with a towel? Why do we put wet washing outside?

Wash the clothes, squeeze them carefully and hang them on the line outside. Let each child feel the wet clothes after they have been washed. Do all the materials hold the same amount of water? Which clothes do they think will dry first and why? What is it outside that helps the clothes to dry?

Next, ask one child to wash the doll's hair. When it is being washed, let everyone see how the water drips off the hair before it has been dried. Now towel-dry it. Is this really dry? Can anyone suggest a way to make it as dry as it was before the wash? How can we re-create the drying conditions found outside? Demonstrate how a hairdryer provides heat and wind in the same way as sunny weather.

Discussion

How do things get dry? Listen to all the children's ideas, testing these out with further questions. Explain that the water held in wet clothes, wet hair and puddles disappears into the air when it is hot or windy as the water changes into vapour – like a boiling kettle.

Follow-up activities

✧ Try 'magic painting' using water on paving stones outside. Watch the pictures disappear as they evaporate in the sun.

✧ Leave a saucer of water outside on a sunny day. Is it still there after an hour or so? Where has the water gone?

✧ Compare the results from a saucer of ordinary water and one with sea (salty) water. The water in both saucers will evaporate but the sea water will leave behind some salt.

✧ Observe raindrops on the window pane. When the weather brightens, look again at the window. Can you still see the raindrops or have they disappeared?

POT-POURRI

Objective

Design and Technology – To make scented bags and practise basic hand/eye co-ordination skills.

Group size

Four children.

What you need

Several large circles of loose-weave material, petals from roses or similarly strong-scented summer flowers, lavender heads, wide-eyed blunt tapestry needles (adult supervision), embroidery thread.

Preparation

Draw around a dinner plate and cut out large circles of the material. Gather a selection of petals and spread these out on a table, together with some coloured threads.

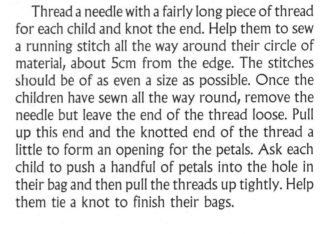

What to do

Explain why people use scents (to make themselves smell attractive). Tell the children that people put pot-pourri bags in drawers of clothes to make these smell fresh and clean. Explain that the children are going to make some of these bags as presents. Let the children smell all the different flower petals and decide which they would like to use for their bags. Let them also choose their material and colour of thread.

Thread a needle with a fairly long piece of thread for each child and knot the end. Help them to sew a running stitch all the way around their circle of material, about 5cm from the edge. The stitches should be of as even a size as possible. Once the children have sewn all the way round, remove the needle but leave the end of the thread loose. Pull up this end and the knotted end of the thread a little to form an opening for the petals. Ask each child to push a handful of petals into the hole in their bag and then pull the threads up tightly. Help them tie a knot to finish their bags.

Discussion

Explain why the children are using blunt needles. Why do you have to be careful with needles? What will happen if you sew too close to the edge of the material? What will happen if you put too many/ too few petals in the bag?

Follow-up activities

✧ Try pressing some petals and flower heads. Does the smell remain after pressing?
✧ With adult help, let the children try to thread a wide-eyed needle with wool or string and sew a pattern on Binca.
✧ Cut 'pretend' petals from folded tissue paper and scent with some of the children's favourite smells (orange, peppermint, chocolate, lemon) by putting a drop of 'smell' on each petal.
✧ Encourage children to learn how to tie their own shoe laces.
✧ Sing together the song 'Pot-pourri' on page 83.

SUN AND SHADE

Objective

History – To learn a little about Victorian attitudes and lifestyle.

Group size

Whole group.

What you need

A sunny day in the playground or park, an umbrella.

Preparation

Make sure all children have adequate protection from the sun and, if you are going away from your usual premises, you will also need to take a first aid bag and have plenty of adult help.

What to do

Talk together about good weather and how the children like to play out of doors when it is warm and sunny. When they get too hot, they probably take some clothes off, protecting their skin with high factor sun cream. Explain that this did not happen in the past as it was not considered 'correct' to remove clothing. Even the children always had to make sure their bodies were covered so children and adults had to find other ways to keep themselves cool.

In the playground or park, point out the sun in the sky, making sure that you warn the children not to look directly at it. Point out that the sun makes everything outside look very bright and clear. Look at the ground. Does it all look the same? Why not? Can the children identify areas which look different? Consider large, dark areas, for instance, those in the shade of a building and look also at dappled areas such as those under trees. These are shady areas. The sunlight has been interrupted by an object such as a person or a tree and this has cast a shadow on the ground.

Ask the children to stand in the sunny area and then put up an umbrella to make the area shady. Which is cooler and which do they prefer if it is very hot weather?

Discussion

In the past, clothing was long-length and long-sleeved. If people stayed in the hot sun, how would they feel? What did they do to keep themselves cool? (Stay in the shade, carry parasols to keep their faces permanently in the shade and use fans.)

In very hot parts of the world, such as India, people often use umbrellas and large fans to keep themselves cool.

Follow-up activities

✧ Look at pictures of Victorian ladies, noting high-necked, long-sleeved, long-length clothing. Role-play being a Victorian lady.
✧ Decorate a small umbrella with lacy material or tassels to make it look like a parasol.
✧ Make a fan by decorating a piece of A4 paper and then folding it, concertina fashion.
✧ Say together the action rhyme 'Sunshine and shadows' on page 69.

I HEAR THUNDER

Objective

Music – To listen carefully to music and to try to re-create the sounds heard.

Group size

Whole group.

What you need

A recording of 'The Pastoral Symphony' 4th movement (the storm before the calm of the happy shepherds' song) by Beethoven, several musical instruments including cymbals, drums, triangles and shakers.

Preparation

Set up the piece of music so that it is ready to play. Place the instruments on a nearby table.

What to do

Read together this poem:
I hear thunder, I hear thunder
Hark, don't you, hark, don't you?
Pitter patter raindrops, pitter patter raindrops
I'm wet through, so are you.

Ask the children to think about all the signs of a thunderstorm approaching and developing, such as black clouds, rumbling thunder, flashes of lightning and the sound of raindrops falling.

Play the music several times for the children and ask them to listen out for all these different sounds. Ask individual children to identify specific signs by raising their hand as they hear it. Can they visualise the other signs such as black clouds and flashes of lightning?

Next, invite them to reproduce the thunderstorm for themselves using some of the available instruments. Crash the cymbals together and bang the drums loudly to make the noise of thunder. Tap gently on the drums with fingertips to produce the sound of drizzle or shake shakers violently to reproduce a soaking downpour. Note the gentleness of the music as the thunder clears away and the weather brightens.

Discussion

How does the music change as the storm develops? What is the first sound of the storm? How do you know the storm is at its height? Which instruments can you identify? Which ones make the loud/soft noises and which the high/low sounds?

Follow-up activities

✧ Listen to other musical representations of storms such as in Haydn's *Creation* – part 1, scene 2 and Rimsky-Korsakov's *Scherezade*. Do the children notice any similarities/differences?
✧ Can the children make some of their own instruments to demonstrate the sounds of the storm? (Try rustling aluminium foil or bursting blown-up paper bags and so on.)
✧ During a thunderstorm, notice how the interval between a flash of lightning and thunder crash lengthens as the storm moves away.
✧ Watch out for signs of an approaching storm by looking at the clouds in the sky.
✧ Read together the poem 'Summer storm' on page 69.

INSECT WORLD

Objective

PE – To improve co-ordination and balancing skills by moving around as various insects.

Group size

Whole group.

What you need

A large, open space, PE cones to resemble flowers and people, large balls for ant food, simple books about insects.

Preparation

Spread out some PE cones around the room, leaving plenty of space around each one.

What to do

Ask the children if they can name any insects. Have they ever watched insects in the summer? Do the insects seem busy? Explain that the children are going to move around, pretending to be insects of various kinds carrying out their daily activities. Divide the children into four groups. Allocate one type of insect to each group – bees, ants, butterflies and wasps. Discuss with each group what they have seen that particular insect do. It may be necessary to help some children with picture books and simple explanations.

Bees buzz slowly and carefully around, collecting pollen from flowers. They store the pollen on their legs, before flying it back to the hive where it is made into honey.

Ants crawl around at great speed, lifting (for them) enormously heavy weights of food. They are very strong.

Butterflies flit gently from flower to flower, feeding and resting in the sunshine. Their wings close as they settle.

Wasps are very active, buzzing aggressively around sweet foods and flying right up to and around people to get what they want.

Having established these general characteristics, encourage each group of children to begin moving in suitable ways to represent their insect, using the props as necessary. Children can use their arms as butterfly wings, opening them when flying and putting them together when resting.

Discussion

Did you buzz slowly and carefully around as a bee? Is it hard work being an ant? How do you feel, flying gently as a butterfly? Are you getting angry being a wasp?

Follow-up activities

✧ Ask children to run as fast as they can on two legs, try crawling as fast on four and imagine running as fast as an ant on six.

✧ Ask them to try squirming along the ground, moving their bodies in waves, like a woodlouse or centipede.

✧ Holding a ball of string or wool, encourage one child at a time to move around various articles in the room, following instructions from the group, so that they spin a 'spider's' web.

✧ Encourage movement as moths; a much busier flight movement, an eagerness to reach the light (ask an adult to hold a yellow 'light' disc) and coming to rest with their wings open.

GOING UP!

Objective

Mathematics — To practise and develop positional language.

Group size

Eight children.

What you need

A large poster of the countryside to pin on the wall. Cut-outs of a hot-air balloon, a flying bird, a horse, a cow, a house and a tree, backed with card and Blu-Tack.

Preparation

Pin up your poster and attach all the cut-out pictures randomly to it. Talk about what the children can see, letting them describe the completed picture in their own words.

What to do

Together with the children, look again at the background scene, identifying specific objects such as hills, fields, clouds, the sun, the sky, flowers and so on. Now look in more detail at the objects that have been added to the picture and describe what you can see. Introduce precise terms such as *beside* the bird and *under* the tree. Demonstrate clearly each new positional word, by pointing to the relevant part of the picture and allow time for the children to absorb the new vocabulary.

Let the children demonstrate their understanding by asking them to take the balloon and put it *down* on the ground. Put it *next to* the flowers and *in front of* the house. As it rises *up* into the sky, put the cow *below* the balloon, the balloon *above* the hills and the sun *behind* the balloon and so on.

Give each child a turn at placing objects correctly according to instructions, using as many different terms as possible.

Discussion

Explain that in our world, all objects are in positions relative to each other. Where is your bedroom in your house? Is it above/below other rooms, next to/in front of the bathroom? When you move about, are you going up/down stairs, beside/under things?

Follow-up activities

✧ How many objects have been added to the poster? Count how many clouds, hills and fields there are.

✧ Play 'Simon says', giving each child a building block and using positional language for the orders: put the block *down* on the ground, *above* your head, *under* your foot and so on.

✧ Think about relative size and height. As the hot-air balloon goes up in the sky, will it look bigger or smaller? Does it really change size?

✧ Think about a big ball rolling towards you. Will it look bigger or smaller as it comes closer?

REFLECTIONS

Objective

English – To practise listening skills and encourage accurate recall by retelling a story.

Group size

Eight children.

What you need

Several postcards or pictures showing reflections, the story 'Mr Rabbit and the moon' on page 82.

Preparation

Show the children the reflection pictures and relate to their own experience by asking whether they have ever looked into still water and seen themselves reflected there or seen scenery re-created in absolutely still water? Point out that reflections show things upside down.

What to do

Sit all the children comfortably around you. Ask for their full attention and then begin to read the story in which Mr Rabbit thinks the moon has fallen out of the sky when he see its reflection in the water. When Mr Rabbit panics at seeing the moon in the water, ask the children whether he needs to worry. What is he actually seeing? Do the children think the characters are being silly or sensible? Why do they think this? The characters saw the moon down in the water but what would they have seen if they had looked up? Make sure that the full meaning of the book is absorbed by all the children.

Then ask each child in turn to re-tell part of the story, using their own words, but making the 'telling' as exciting and expressive as possible. If a part of the story is missed out by any particular child, allow them to continue with what they are saying but then ask the group whether they remember it in that way too. If no one can produce the correct sequence of events, tell them what you remember and ask whether they think that is right.

Discussion

Do you like this story? Who is your favourite character? Why? If you had seen Mr Rabbit worrying, what would you have done?

Follow-up activities

✧ When you read the story, use a different voice for each character. Try saying something new in the same voice. Can the children identify the different characters?
✧ Play three different musical instruments in sequence. Can the children remember the order in which you play them?
✧ Ask the children to tell you a well-known story without first reading it to them. Encourage a high degree of accuracy and detail.
✧ Play a memory game which involves careful listening to unexpected facts. Include a pink giraffe, a thin elephant and a spotted tiger for example!
✧ Complete the photocopiable sheet on page 88.

CHAPTER 2
THE SUN

Looking at the Sun's central role in the universe and its undoubted power, children consider its effects on plants, on various food items and on their bodies in this chapter. Sunsets are re-created, Midsummer Day is linked to looking at an ancient monument and hot, dry climates are considered.

GIVE ME SUNSHINE

Objective
Science – To explore the need for sunlight for plants to grow healthily.

Group size
Whole group.

What you need
Sunflower seeds, small plastic flower pots, compost, flat tray, spoon, sticky labels, plastic jug and water.

Preparation
Protect the floor from spillages. Put out the flower pots and label several 'light' and the others 'dark'. Put the compost in a large flat container using an old spoon. Fill the jug with water.

What to do
Start by asking if any of the children have grown a plant from seed. Explain that together you are going to find out what healthy plants need to make them grow well. Give each child a flower pot of their own, together with two sunflower seeds. Help them to fill their pot about two thirds of the way up with compost. Ask each child to plant their seeds by pushing them down gently into the compost. What will you need to do next in order for your seeds to grow?

Encourage suggestions, especially those focusing on watering the seeds, giving them plenty of light and keeping them warm. What else will your seeds need to grow healthily?

Conduct an experiment by inviting several of the children to keep their pots in a dark place and the others to put theirs on a sunny windowsill. Make sure that the children understand that they are responsible for looking after their own plants, ensuring they are watered enough but not too much. After a couple of weeks, compare the two sets of plants. The ones in the dark should have yellow leaves with long, thin, white stems. The plants kept in the sun should look strong and green.

Discussion
What do you think will happen to the plants which are always in the dark? How will the seeds in the sunny place grow? Which will be stronger? How can you tell whether the plant is healthy?

Follow-up activities
✧ Plant a bulb in compost and keep it in the dark until a shoot begins to grow. Take it out into the light and watch the yellow shoot turn green.
✧ Transfer a small, flowering house plant out of the light into a dark cupboard for a few days. Watch the plant start to look very unhappy and its leaves begin to turn yellow. Put the plant back into the light and (hopefully!) watch it return to health.

MELTING POWER!

Objective

Science — To examine how a variety of everyday substances change in the hot sunshine.

Group size

Whole group.

What you need

A small bar of chocolate, a lump of butter, ice cubes, a bowl of jelly, a saucer of milk, lettuce leaves, a slice of bread, a hot sunny day.

Preparation

Gather all the substances together and find a safe spot outside where these can be left for a few hours without being disturbed.

What to do

Talk about how we use fridges and freezers at home and about the need to keep food out of direct sunlight in order to keep it fresh. Explain that you are going to conduct an experiment to find out what happens if food is not kept cool.

Distribute the food and ask the children to take it outside to the designated sunny spot, under adult supervision. Ask for predictions about what will happen to the food after it has been outside in the sun for a while. After an hour or so, depending on the strength of the sun, return to the site and see whether the children's predictions were correct. The chocolate, ice cubes, butter and jelly should have melted, the bread should have started to go hard, the lettuce limp and the milk solid.

Discussion

Why have the substances changed in this way? How was the jelly made? The ice and the jelly have reverted to their original states. If chilled again, they will change back to set jelly and ice. Can we get the fresh bread, lettuce and milk back to their original state or have they changed for ever?

Follow-up activities

✧ Ask the children to hold their favourite chocolate bar (in its wrapper) in their hand for a minute or two. Unwrap it and see what has happened. Why?
✧ Cool down the butter and chocolate again. What happens? Do they look the same as before? How are they different?
✧ Complete the photocopiable sheet on page 89.
✧ Leave a picked flower in the sun for a few hours. Watch how it goes limp and the stem bends over as it loses water.

IN SPACE!

Objective

PE — To follow instructions for movement.

Group size

Whole group.

What you need

A room with plenty of space for the children to move around, information books about the solar system.

Preparation

Ask all the children to spread out and sit down in a space.

What to do

Talk about the solar system with the children. Explain that the Earth Is a planet and the Sun is a huge star. There are nine main planets in our solar system including ours — the Earth — and these all move in their own circles around the Sun. The Moon goes round the Earth as the Earth circles the Sun.

Explain that the children are going to move around like planets in the solar system. Start by talking about the Moon circling the Earth. Let one child be the Earth while others pretend to be the Moon moving in a circle around him/her.

Next, talk about all the planets which circle the Sun. They are called Mercury, Venus, Earth, Mars, Jupiter, Saturn, Uranus, Neptune and Pluto. Mercury is closest to the Sun and Pluto is furthest away. The planets nearest to the Sun move much more quickly than those which are further away. Choose a child to represent the Sun. First, ask the children to move in a circle around the Sun quite fast like Earth and Mars. Then let them be like Neptune or Pluto, moving at a snail's pace. Follow up by asking them to move very fast like Mercury and Venus or slowly like Jupiter, Saturn and Uranus. Repeat, letting different children be the Sun and Earth.

Discussion

How do you move very fast? Is it difficult to move at a snail's pace? What animals can you think of which move very fast (mice, cheetahs), slowly (elephants, hippos) and which move at a snail's pace (snail, sloth)?

What is in the middle of our solar system? What goes around the Sun? What goes around the Earth? Which planet is closest to the Sun and which is furthest away?

Follow-up activities

✧ Listen to Gustav Holst's *The Planets* and let the children move to match the music.
✧ Encourage the children to follow a drum beat which varies in speed, by marching in time to it.
✧ Pretend to be spacemen walking in heavy spacesuits, and then rockets shooting off into the sky, going to the moon.

STONEHENGE

Objective

History – To learn about an ancient monument.

Group size

Whole group.

What you need

A carpeted area, postcards and books about Stonehenge.

Preparation

Sit everyone down on the carpeted area. Have Stonehenge material available close by.

What to do

Explain that the children are going to think about this ancient monument because of its connection to Midsummer Day. In the summer, days are long and it gets dark much later at night. Midsummer Day is the day of the year when it is light for the longest time.

Now ask the children whether they know anything abut Stonehenge. Start by discussing old buildings in general terms. Consider castles and cathedrals. Have the children made visits to these? Have they all been complete or were some in ruins? Discuss what this means.

Look at pictures of Stonehenge. Discuss the pattern of stones they see (some more than 4,000 years old) and point out that if you stand in the very middle of the stone circle and look towards the entrance, you will see the Sun rise exactly in line with the entrance, on Midsummer Day. Introduce the various theories about why Stonehenge was built and why the position of the stones and circles is as it is. Some people believe Stonehenge was a temple, used for worship and some, that it may have been used to tell the time or to look at the movements of the Sun and the Moon.

As this is quite sophisticated subject matter you will obviously need to base the level of your discussion on the attention level and abilities of your children, developing the facts as the children show interest.

Discussion

How do you think the people who built Stonehenge managed to move those huge stones (some are taller than double decker buses)? (They rolled some of the stones, used levers underneath them and dragged some using ropes.) Look how the elements (sun, rain and wind) have 'weathered' the stones, just like stones on the beach.

Follow-up activities

✧ Give the children some clay and ask them to make some of the shapes seen at Stonehenge. Help them to arrange these into the shape remaining at the monument today.

✧ Look at pictures and postcards of other ruins such as castles.

✧ How do we learn about something as old as Stonehenge, built such a very long time ago? Discuss sources of evidence (photographs, books and archaeological digs).

✧ Encourage the children to keep diaries of important events in their lives so others, who were not there, can learn about them.

✧ If you live anywhere near Stonehenge, try to arrange a visit.

SUNBURN

Objective

Design and Technology – To design and make a sun-hat.

Group size

Four children.

What you need

Scissors, glue, sugar paper, stapler (for adult use), pencils, dinner plates and side plates.

Preparation

Draw around the dinner plate, place the side plate in the centre of the large circle and draw around the side plate. Cut out a 10cm wide band, long enough to go round a child's head and a rectangle for the back flap of the hat. Make enough for each child. Have all the other equipment available on a table nearby.

What to do

Explain that the children are going to make a hat which will protect them from burning in the sun. Discuss the various features required:

● a top to protect the scalp
● a front peak to protect the eyes
● a back flap to protect the neck.

Ask the children to carefully cut out the large, circular shape and to cut slits, about 2cm apart, up to the smaller, circular shape inside. Fold these flaps downwards. Position the 10cm band to surround this circular shape and staple it together. Ask the children to glue the flaps, push them down inside the band and stick them firmly in place, thus making a pill-box shape hat.

Help the children to draw around the side plate again and cut out this shape. Fold it in half to form a semicircle and glue both sides together. Draw a line about 2cm from the straight edge and cut strips up to this line. Fold the strips over downwards, glue them and stick them firmly onto the hat band to make a peak. Cut out a rectangle of sugar paper and glue this onto the back of the hat to form a flap to protect the neck.

Discussion

The sun can burn the skin very quickly. What precautions do we need to take? Why do we put on sun cream and sun-hats? What other things can we do to protect ourselves from the sun? (Cover up in light, cool clothing.)

Follow-up activities

✦ Design loose-fitting cover-up garments using old cotton sheeting.
✦ Recite the poem 'Cover up' on page 68 and sing the song 'In the heat' on page 84.

THE SUN HAS GOT HIS HAT ON

Objective

Music — To develop a sense of rhythm while creating a dance about the sun.

Group size

Whole group.

What you need

Plenty of room for the children to move around, tapes of happy and sad music, floaty scarves, a pretty sun hat, a tape recorder and a recording of the song 'The sun has got his hat on'.

Preparation

Sit the children down in a large space in your room. Set up the tape recorder and assemble all the music together.

What to do

Listen to a selection of the music with the children, mentioning how some music sounds sad and some happy. Now play through 'The sun has got his hat on'. Is this a happy or sad piece of music? Explain that the group is going to make up their own dance to this music.

Ask the children to clap in time to the music, establishing a beat of four claps for each line of the song. Start to structure the dance by suggesting the children get in a circle (as clouds), around one child (the sun — with his hat on!). Ask the children to move slowly round in a circle in time to the music — four steady steps. At a suitable point in the music — 'and he's coming out today', ask the child who is the sun to break out from the circle,

revealing himself in his full glory. If possible, give each child a floaty scarf to raise above their heads each time there is a 'hip, hip, hip hooray'.

As the children become more confident about moving in time to the beat, try increasing the tempo so that they are moving at twice the speed; with eight claps to each line of the song.

Discussion

What makes the music sound happy? Is the music fast or slow, loud or soft, high or low? Which instruments are playing? What things make you feel happy or sad? How do you move when you are happy or sad?

Follow-up activities

◇ Encourage careful listening to a drum beat by asking children to clap in time as you vary the speed.

◇ Tap out the rhythm of a familiar nursery rhyme with your fingers. Can the children identify it without hearing the music?

◇ Ask the children to try conducting by moving their hands up and down in time to the music. For some music they will need to 'draw' a triangle shape in the air in order to keep in time (for three beats).

RED SKY AT NIGHT

Objective

Art – To re-create beautiful sunsets using a variety of techniques.

Group size

Six children.

What you need

Large sheets of white paper or card, brushes, red, orange, yellow, blue, purple and white poster paint and chalks, sponges, black felt-tipped pens, postcards or pictures of sunsets, tissue paper in 'sunset' colours, PVA glue, newspaper.

Preparation

Cover tables with newspaper and spread out the different media, giving the children as much space as possible to work.

What to do

Gather the children together and talk about sunsets. Have any of the children ever seen a sunset? Look at the pictures and postcards and talk about the beautiful colours seen. Explain that they are going to make their own 'red' skies.

Let the children experiment with the different media to create the desired effect.

Try these techniques:

● Paint bands of colour onto the card or paper, blending them together by using very watery paint or by washing over with water afterwards.

● Use chalks on their side to produce bands of colour and blend or 'smudge' these using the sponges.

● Tear strips of tissue paper from the variety of colours and stick these, using PVA glue so that they overlap onto the paper or card to create the effects seen in a real sunset. Make light colours by using only one layer of tissue and more intense colours by using several thicknesses.

Look again at the pictures and postcards of the sunsets and identify dark, silhouette shapes. Reproduce these on the children's sunset pictures by drawing and inking in black shapes with the felt-tipped pens.

Make a stunning display with the children's finished work.

Discussion

Talk about different shades of the same colour. How can you make a darker red, a lighter orange a deep purple? What happens to the bands of colour as they mix?

Follow-up activities

◇ Use water colours as a different medium and let the children experiment with making much 'gentler' pictures.

◇ Gather a selection of old cards and magazines together. Cut out small pieces of red, orange, purple and yellow of various shades and stick these together to make another sunset picture.

◇ Learn and recite the rhyme 'Red sky at night, shepherds' delight, Red sky in the morning, shepherds' warning'. Explain how the colours that we see in the sky can be a very clear indication of the weather to come.

TOO HOT!

Objective

Geography – To learn about the climate in the desert.

Group size

Whole group.

What you need

A globe, information books/pictures about the desert, a sunny day.

Preparation

Sit all the children down in a circle so that they can all see the globe, pictures and books.

What to do

Take the children outside early in the morning when the sun has not been up for long and let them feel the temperature. Do they need to wear a jumper? Take them outside again in the middle of the day or early in the afternoon, when the sun is directly overhead. Is it warmer or colder? Do they still need to wear a jumper?

Look carefully at the globe, explaining that it represents the world in which we live. Tell the children that the green parts of the globe are land and the blue parts are sea. Locate Great Britain on the globe. The land at the very top of the globe is called the North Pole and the land at the bottom is called the South Pole. The Poles are the coldest parts of the world.

The very middle of the globe is called the equator and countries in this part of the world are the hottest because the sun shines directly overhead for a very long time each day. This is where the deserts are.

Explain that deserts consist of sand, sometimes blown into dunes or hills by the strong desert winds. They are very dry places and only special plants called cacti, which can store water in their stems, survive. Camels are well adapted to live in the desert. They store lots of fat in their hump and can go without food and water for a long time as they cross the barren land.

Discussion

What other animals live in the desert? What is it like at night in the desert? Does it ever rain? What does the desert look like after a rainstorm?

Follow-up activities

✧ Look in more detail at books about camels to find out how well adapted they are to desert life (thick, hairy skins to keep them cool in the day and warm at night, wide feet for walking on sand, lots of hairs around their eyes, closing nostrils for protection during sandstorms and tough, hairy lips for eating scrub).
✧ Make desert snakes by carefully cutting around a spiral drawn onto card. Decorate them.
✧ If possible, look at some real desert plants. Warn the children not to touch!
✧ Complete the photocopiable on page 90.
✧ Read the poem 'A letter to the grown-ups' on page 67.

CHAPTER 3
OUTDOOR ACTIVITIES

Children learn to use their bodies and all their senses to explore sand, listen to brass bands, set up their own summer fête and take part in races and cycling activities in this chapter. They will also learn how to look after themselves outside and how others celebrate an important event.

SANDCASTLES

Objective

Science – To examine the properties of wet (damp) and dry sand.

Group size

Eight children.

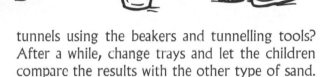

What you need

Two sand trays (one filled with wet sand and the other with dry), spades, rakes, sieves, tunnelling tools, different sized beakers, magnifying glasses.

Preparation

Divide your group into two with four children by each sand tray. Put some 'tools' in each tray.

What to do

Explain that many of us come across sand in the summer – on the beach, at the seaside. The children are going to find out about sand by experimenting with it in the sand trays.

Start by examining the sand with magnifying glasses. Can the children see individual grains of sand? What has happened to the grains in the wet sand? Encourage experimentation. Think about such things as texture and colour. How would you describe the sand? Draw out such words as sticky, messy, grainy, tickly, soft and so on. Next, ask them to push the sand up into a mound. Will it keep this shape? For how long? Drop a handful of sand from a height of about 30cm into the tray. Describe the noise it makes. Try sieving a handful of sand. Will it go through the sieve? Why/why not? Can you make a castle with towers and

tunnels using the beakers and tunnelling tools? After a while, change trays and let the children compare the results with the other type of sand.

Discussion

What is dry sand? How is the wet sand different? The individual, dry grains of sand will go through the holes of a sieve but they won't stick together to make shapes, whereas the bulk of wet sand won't go through small holes but it will stick together and retain its shape.

Follow-up activities

✧ Learn the song 'The wise man and the foolish man' (*Okki-tokki-unga*, A & C Black) in which the wise man built his house on rock and the foolish man built his house on sand. Whose house would last the longest?
✧ Discuss how sand is formed. Rocks are constantly battered against each other by the waves crashing on the beach. This breaks them up into smaller and smaller pieces and eventually, the tiny particles of sand.
✧ Make 'sand' pictures by 'drawing' in glue on a piece of card and sprinkling this with dry sand, shaking off the excess. Could you use wet sand?
✧ Using a beam balance, compare the weights of a beaker of wet and dry sand. Why is the wet sand heavier? (Show how heavy water is by letting the children lift a small bucket of water.)

READY, STEADY, GO!

Objective

PE — To develop physical co-ordination and co-operative skills.

Group size

Whole group.

What you need

A nice day and a grassy area with plenty of space for running around, PE cones, big footballs, cardboard rolls, beanbags, two adults, two stopwatches.

Preparation

If you are planning to go away from the premises, make sure you have sufficient adult help, first aid and sun protection. Put out a 'finishing cone' for each team.

What to do

Start by dividing your group into two teams, trying to maintain a fairly even balance of speed and general athletic ability. Explain that you are going to play some team games and that every member of the team must try their very best for themselves and for their team. Give special encouragement to try to improve the children's individual performances.

Ask the children to line up one behind the other. Begin with a simple relay race where they pass a cardboard roll between team members. Explain that each competitor has to run round an agreed mark, run back to their team and pass the roll to the next person, before joining the back of the line.

Having established the basic rules, increase the complexity of the races gradually.

Ideas could include:

● running to the mark and hopping back to the team, touching the next person gently on the shoulder

● big strides to the mark, small steps back

● arranging the remaining cones to make a 'slalom' which team members have to weave between

● dribbling a ball to the mark and back

● walking with a beanbag on their head to the mark, returning with it in their hand.

When performing some of these more complicated manoeuvres, see if individual children can improve their 'personal best' times by timing two attempts.

Discussion

How can we help our team? If you are not watching, will you know when to go? How can you get back to your team faster? Do you need to run right past the cone?

Follow-up activities

Gather each team in a circle with their adult and assign a number to each member before these activities:

✧ Encourage careful listening by explaining that when you call their number they have to run around the circle and back to their place. Call all numbers in random order. The first team to finish is the winner.

✧ Throw a football to individual team members in order. Teams score a point for each caught ball. After three or four rounds, compare scores. Have individual children improved their own catching skills?

TAKE CARE!

Objective

RE – To make rules together for keeping safe.

Group size

Whole group.

What you need

A day or days when the group is leaving the premises to go on a summer visit.

Preparation

Set aside time for the following discussion before embarking on the visit. Make sure you have adequate adult help, sun protection and first aid.

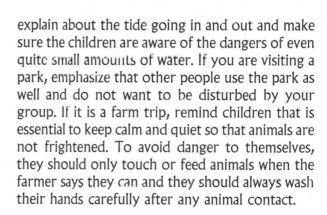

What to do

Summer is a time when children often leave their immediate premises to go out on trips. Explain that to keep them safe it is necessary to draw up rules. Rules are needed to cover all aspects of the trip including the journey there.

Begin by drawing up general rules for good behaviour while in transit: be quiet, listen carefully, don't throw things, walk, don't run and so on. What dangers might you encounter? Discuss traffic and crossing roads. Where should you cross? What should you do before, and as you cross? (Cross at a zebra crossing if possible or on a clear stretch of road. Hold an adult's hand. Stop, look and listen.)

When they have arrived at their destination, talk about the importance of staying close to the adults looking after them and not wandering off or talking to strangers. If they are at the seaside,

explain about the tide going in and out and make sure the children are aware of the dangers of even quite small amounts of water. If you are visiting a park, emphasize that other people use the park as well and do not want to be disturbed by your group. If it is a farm trip, remind children that is essential to keep calm and quiet so that animals are not frightened. To avoid danger to themselves, they should only touch or feed animals when the farmer says they can and they should always wash their hands carefully after any animal contact.

Discussion

Include the children in all the discussions, for example, what rules should we have in the park? (Only run between this tree and the fence, don't go near any picnics, be careful of the flowers, look where you are going.) What would happen if we didn't have rules? (People might get hurt and lost and environments might be damaged.)

Follow-up activities

✧ Draw pictures of 'dos' and 'don'ts' for various environments.
✧ Practise crossing an imaginary road. Hold hands, stop, look and listen. Then walk straight across, looking and listening as you cross.
✧ Photocopy page 91 and let the children cut out the pictures and put them in the right order.
✧ Invite a police officer to visit your group and sensitively discuss potentially dangerous situations.

BANDSTAND

Objective

Music – To learn about brass instruments and listen to the sounds they make.

Group size

Eight children.

What you need

Cardboard rolls, thin card, stapler, masking tape, scissors, a dinner plate and a side plate, pictures of brass instruments (or, if possible, a real brass instrument), a tape recorder and a recording of some brass band music, such as some marches by Sousa, dressing-up clothes.

Preparation

Sit the children beside you. Have both tape recorder and tapes within easy reach, together with any instruments you have available.

What to do

Listen to some of the brass band music together. Have any of the children heard this sort of band playing before? It is a summery sound because it reminds us of bands playing in bandstands in the park in the summer and soldiers playing while marching on parade outside. Look closely at the pictures of the brass instruments. What are they made of? Can you identify the different parts – the mouthpiece which the player blows through, the tubes and valves which form the body of the trumpet and the bell where the sound comes out?

Make your own pretend instruments for a brass band summer parade.

Give each child a cardboard tube. Help them to draw carefully around a dinner and a side plate on to the thin card and carefully cut out these circles. Make one cut from the edge of the circle into the middle, roll up and staple into cones. Insert into the cardboard tube, using the larger, loosely-rolled cone as the bell and the smaller, tightly-rolled one as the mouthpiece. Secure carefully with masking tape. The children could paint their trumpets golden yellow, leaving the mouthpieces unpainted.

Let the children dress up and parade up and down outside, with their brass band instruments. Perform by 'blowing' the trumpets while humming an agreed tune into them.

Discussion

Can you name any brass instruments? (Trumpet, trombone, French horn and so on.) Do you like the sound of the brass band? How does it make you feel? Has anyone seen a brass band playing in a bandstand in the park.

Follow-up activities

✧ Discuss other types of instruments – woodwind, strings and percussion. Can you name any of these? Play some percussion instruments (drums, cymbals, triangles) to compare and contrast the sounds.

✧ Let the children take it in turns to be the conductor of their brass band. Agree a tune they will all try to 'play' on their instruments and let the chosen child use their hands to beat in time, either up and down (for two beats) or by 'drawing' a triangle in the air (for three beats).

INDEPENDENCE DAY

Objective

RE – To learn about an important celebration in another country.

Group size

Whole group.

What you need

Real flags and bunting or tissue paper to make your own, streamers, frieze paper, balloons, scissors, wool, felt-tipped pens, poster paints and paintbrushes, dressing-up clothes and hats, food and plates for a small tea party.

Preparation

Set out all the resources you have gathered together on two long tables.

What to do

Explain that this celebration takes place in North America. Find the United States of America on a map of the world. Tell the children that Independence Day is celebrated on 4 July and commemorates the day in 1776 when the USA became independent. This day is a public holiday in the USA and there is no school that day. Families celebrate together with all sorts of outdoor activities. Streets are decorated with flags and banners and there are pageants to watch and parades to take part in. Everyone enjoys firework displays in the evening.

Ask the children to prepare an outside area for their own Independence Day celebration. Hang up balloons and thin streamers. Let the children decorate the frieze paper with pens or paint to make banners and fix these close to your party area. String up your flags if you have any. If not, make a string of bunting by cutting squares of tissue paper and taping these to a length of wool, in order to hang them up. Let the children dress up and wear commercial or home-made hats in order to stage their own celebratory parade. Include an area for party food and have a small tea party after the parade.

Discussion

Have you ever been to similar celebrations? When and where? Did you dress up or take part in parades? Did you eat special food? Have you seen any firework displays?

Follow-up activities

✧ Talk about birthdays as other forms of celebration.
✧ Explain to the children about Tuan Yang Chieh – the Chinese Dragon Boat Festival – when rowing races are held in beautifully carved, dragon-head boats to remember the wise adviser and poet, Qu Yuan.
✧ Discuss Raksha Bandhan, a Hindu Festival, when brotherly and sisterly love is celebrated and people think about caring for and protecting others.
✧ Tell the children the story of St Swithin and the associated theory that if it rains on St Swithin's Day (15 July), it will then rain continuously for forty days.
✧ Sing the song 'Summer street party' on page 86 and say the poem 'Carnival' on page 75.

ON YOUR BIKE

Objective

PE – To practise balancing and linking a series of actions which imitate the movements of a bicycle.

Group size

Whole group.

What you need

A large open space outside on a nice day.

Preparation

Ask all the children to find a space and a partner.

What to do

Talk about outdoor activities which people like to do in the summer and bicycling in particular. When the days get longer and it is warmer, people want to be outside and bicycling is a favourite pastime. Can any of the children ride bicycles? Did they start by having stabilizers?

Explain that they are going to pretend to ride bikes, imitating the various movements required. Start by asking one child of each pair to put their hands on their partner's shoulders. Ask them to try to balance on one leg and then the other while holding on. Then try to balance without holding on. Compare the feeling to riding their bike with and without stabilisers (their partner).

Next, ask the children to pretend to work the pedals by slowly raising each leg in turn and pressing down with their foot as they return it to the ground. Complete the session by asking the children to make bicycling movements with their arms, pushing and pulling the air, instead of the pedals and chain.

Discussion

What do you need to be able to do in order to ride a bicycle successfully? (Grip handlebars, balance, push and pull pedals.) Why is it easier to ride tricycles or bicycles with stabilizers?

Follow-up activities

✧ Try to make hoops roll in the same way as the wheels of a bicycle by balancing them carefully and pushing them gently at the side.

✧ Look at pictures of circus stunt cycles and penny-farthings and imagine riding one of these. Try balancing activities (for instance, standing on one leg on a low bench) of increasing difficulty with plenty of adult supervision.

✧ Ask the children to get into a circle and then an oval by joining hands. Drop hands. Now ask them to put their hands on the child in front's shoulders. They should now all follow the child in front, moving slowly at first and then more quickly, pretending to be the chain on a bicycle.

✧ Pretend to be the tyres on a bicycle. Lie on the floor, being flat tyres, as air is pumped in the children begin to grow, gradually increasing in size until they are stretching up high.

SUMMER FÊTE

Objective

Mathematics – To practise mathematical skills at a pretend summer fête.

Group size

Eight children.

What you need

A suitable outdoor area, several small tables, a small teddy, a beam balance, some building blocks of various sizes, different lengths of wool of assorted colours, scissors, a small plastic, see-through jar full of wrapped sweets.

Preparation

Set up the corner with small tables on which you should place the three games:
● estimate the length of the wool
● guess the weight of the teddy
● guess how many sweets in the jar.
   Decorate the area with balloons and streamers.

What to do

Ask the children if they have ever been to a summer fête. What stalls were there? Tell the children that they are going to practise estimating skills at the stalls of their own pretend fête.

Introduce the three games that they will play at these stalls. Set up the first game by putting the teddy on one of the tables, together with the selection of building blocks and the beam balance. Explain the rules. One at a time, children should handle the teddy and then estimate his weight by trying to place an equivalent weight of building blocks into one of the cups of the balance. Check the guesses by putting the teddy into the other cup and seeing what happens.

For the second game, cut various lengths of different coloured wool and stretch these out randomly on another table. The children have to look at these pieces of wool and estimate which is the longest. They can test their guesses at the end by laying the pieces side by side.

In the final game, ask the children to guess how many sweets are in the jar. Again, they can test their guesses by counting them at the end.

Discussion

When you have put things in both cups of the beam balance, what does it do? What does this mean?

Follow-up activities

✧ Use toy money and let the children pay for using the stalls. Set prices according to your supply of money! Count up the takings at the end of the day.
✧ Put out three beakers of different shapes. Which will hold the most water? Compare volumes by pouring from one container to another.
✧ Play skittles, using skittles marked 1–6. Encourage the children to add up their scores, using small bricks if necessary. Who is the winner?
✧ Make a few 'prizes' out of construction kits. Hand these out to the 'winners'.
✧ Say together the rhyme 'Our school fête' on page 75.

WHAT IS HAPPENING?

Objective

English – To recognize the word ending and identify the sound '-ing' in words.

Group size

Whole group.

What you need

A few simple story books with plenty of action, using '-ing' words, such as *My Cat Jack* Patricia Casey (Walker Books).

Preparation

You need the children's full attention so make sure they are sitting comfortably and are quiet before you begin.

What to do

Ask the children to close their eyes and imagine what they see, hear, smell, touch and taste during the summer, when they are out in the park, at the seaside or in the country. Can they see flowers growing, people bicycling, children running, birds flying, boats sailing and horses galloping? Can they hear bees buzzing, aeroplanes roaring, children laughing, ducks quacking, people talking and seagulls crying? Can they smell barbecues or roses? Perhaps they are touching hot sand or fresh green grass and they could be tasting strawberries and ice-cream.

Emphasize all the '-ing' words as you say them. Now ask the children if they can think of other things they will be doing during the course of the day – washing, eating, drinking, sleeping, swimming, picnicking, reading, writing, playing, walking, talking and so on. As the children come up with all these words, encourage them to realize how important this word ending is.

Finally, ask all the children to go on an '-ing' hunt, looking in any of the books for as many of these words as they can find.

Discussion

What kind of words are '-ing' words? (Doing words – something is always happening.)

Follow-up activities

✧ Can the children think of some 'th-ing-s', by adding one letter to the '-ing' ending? Encourage words such as king, ring, sing and wing. Emphasize the rhymes.

✧ As they read to you, take every opportunity to point out both types of '-ing' words, 'doing' words and individual objects.

✧ Let the children tell you a story using as many '-ing' words as they can. They could start with an introduction such as – 'The king was singing. He was wearing a ring.' or 'The bird was not flying. His wing was hurting.'

CHAPTER 4
SUMMER FOOD

Handle, examine, smell and taste a variety of summer food in this chapter. Children can express their likes and dislikes, learn about what happens at modern 'Pick your own' farms and contrast this with the lack of fresh produce in the past. Finally, they will be asked to design and write an invitation for a summer barbecue.

STRAWBERRY FAIR?

Objective

Mathematics – To encourage mathematical investigation, taking into account, size, number and weight.

Group size

Whole group; in pairs.

What you need

A beam balance (with individual buckets), one or two punnets of strawberries of varying sizes (depending on the size of your group).

Preparation

Explain that on this occasion, the strawberries are not for eating! Tell the children how easily strawberries can be squashed and encourage very gentle handling. Explain and demonstrate how the beam balance works. Check with parents for any strawberry allergies.

What to do

Explain to the children that strawberries are only plentiful in the summer and are very expensive at other times of the year. Therefore they are a great treat in the summer time. Ask the children if they have ever eaten strawberries. Do they like them? (Hopefully, all of the children will like them!)

Ask the children to imagine that they have been given a punnet of strawberries to share with their partner. Ask the first pair of children to place a few strawberries in each bucket. Have they put the same number in each bucket? Will the beam balance or will it settle one way or the other? What

does this mean? Which bucket of strawberries is heavier? Which bucket contains most fruit? Is this the heaviest bucket?

Invite the next pair of children to try to redress or keep the balance by adding a few more strawberries. Encourage the children to think beyond the numbers involved to the size (and therefore weight) of individual strawberries. Continue in this way until each pair of children has had a turn. Is the end result a more or less balanced pair of buckets? If not, ask the last pair of children to try to rectify this situation. (If they are struggling, suggest that they might try moving a very small strawberry from one side to the other.) Count the number of strawberries in each bucket – hopefully the number will be different!

Discussion

When the beam balance is level, the two buckets weigh the same. However, this does not necessarily mean that each will have the same number of strawberries. Are you surprised by this? Can you suggest reasons why it is not always the bucket with the greatest number of strawberries that is the heaviest?

Follow-up activities

✧ Provide a blunt knife and two strawberries of different sizes. Can the children suggest a way to 'be fair'. Check, using the balance.
✧ Try to balance real and 'pretend' strawberries, made from modelling dough.
✧ Use the photocopiable page 92 to count the number of hidden strawberries.
✧ Ask the children to examine their hands after this activity. Why are they red?
✧ If the strawberries are in a fit state, wash and puree them with a little sugar and add them to milk or lemonade. Drink!
✧ Recite the poem 'Strawberry pie' on page 72.

PICNIC SANDWICHES

Objective

Design and Technology – To design and make a sandwich for summer.

Group size

Four children.

What you need

Brown and white thin-sliced bread, easy-spread butter or margarine, a selection of salad vegetables, summer fruits, savoury spreads and jams, blunt knives, chopping boards, tables.

Preparation

Spread out the various sandwich ingredients on child-sized tables, together with chopping boards and knives. Make sure all the children wash their hands very carefully in preparation for handling the food.

What to do

Explain that the children are going to make their own sandwiches for a summer picnic. Encourage them to think carefully about the various flavours they have in front of them. Talk especially about the summer fruits and vegetables which are readily available at this time of year.

Let them choose ingredients for their sandwiches, starting with the type of bread that they would like to use. When choosing, encourage the children to think about such things as:
● The texture of their sandwich – if they put too many things inside it, it will be very difficult to handle and eat. If they use too many 'wet' ingredients, the bread will collapse.
● The colours in their sandwich – too many green things could make it look uninteresting.
● The smell of their sandwich – a delicious smell will make the sandwich even more appealing.
● Its overall taste – encourage adventurous mixing of a variety of tastes.

Having chosen the various ingredients, let the children assemble their sandwiches by spreading the bread, chopping the food and closing the sandwich. Finish by helping them to cut their sandwiches into halves, quarters or triangle shapes.

Discussion

Why do we eat sandwiches in the summer? Encourage a discussion about warm weather, eating cold food and transporting food outside to eat, using insulated picnic bags and thermos flasks to keep it cool.

Follow-up activities

✧ Eat the sandwiches as part of your Independence Day (page 31) tea party!
✧ Explore other sandwich possibilities, for example, pitta bread, rice cakes, crackers, baguettes and rolls.
✧ Ask the children to think about other suitable picnic food, such as cold sausages, small buns, tomatoes, hard-boiled eggs, crisps and so on. What makes them suitable for a picnic?
✧ Talk about transporting drinks easily, without spilling them. Which type of container is the most practical for this purpose? Consider glass and plastic bottles, cartons and foil bags. What happens if you do not want to drink the whole drink at once? Which would be the best container to use?

ICE-CREAMS

Objective

Mathematics – To become familiar with bar charts as a way of recording information.

Group size

Whole group.

What you need

Big building blocks, a whiteboard, a marker pen, a large piece of card, felt-tipped pens and pictures of several popular kinds of ice-cream.

Preparation

Clear a space on the floor so that you can gather the group around you in a circle. Put the board, blocks and writing materials within easy reach and in a spot where everyone can see them.

What to do

Talk about ice-creams and how refreshing they are on a hot day. Where can you buy them? How many different kinds can you name? Does everyone like the same ice-cream? Explain that you are going to try to find out which is the most popular ice-cream by asking the children their favourites and recording who likes what as a bar chart.

Demonstrate what a bar chart looks like by using the building blocks to record how many girls, boys and adults there are in the room, using one block for each person and building separate towers for girls, boys and teachers. Then transfer this information onto a bar chart drawn on the board. Which is the highest tower and therefore which group has the most?

When the children have got the general idea, start making a bar chart of favourite ice-creams which can be used as a display. Draw or paste pictures of the various ice-creams along the bottom of the display paper. Take votes for each kind and record the results by drawing or pasting the correct number of similar ice-creams in a tower against each item. The finished bar chart should give a good indication of which flavours the children prefer.

Discussion

Ask the children to explain what the bar chart means. Can they count and write down the numbers in each column? Discuss mathematical language, such as more/less, greater/smaller to help their basic understanding of number order.

Follow-up activities

✦ Give the children their own squared paper to do surveys and make bar charts of other summer favourites, for example ice lolly flavours or fruits.
✦ When the weather is very hot, do the children prefer to eat ice-cream or drink an ice-cold drink? Test guesses against facts.
✦ Let the children experiment with other ways of recording. For example, draw an ice-cream and a drink in different circles and draw pictures of people in the circle of their choice.
✦ Sing the song 'Sun and sand' on page 85 and recite the rhyme 'Sticky licky' on page 71.

TUTTI FRUTTI

Objective

Science — To examine different summer fruits carefully, using all the senses.

Group size

Eight children.

What you need

A selection of refreshing and juicy summer fruits (melon, peach, strawberry, raspberry, gooseberry, pineapple, cherry), blunt knives, chopping boards.

Preparation

Spread out the selection of fruit on long tables and put the knives and chopping boards within easy reach. Make sure all the children wash their hands prior to handling the fruit.

What to do

Start with a general discussion about what fruit is. All fruit contains seeds or stones and, when planted, these seeds grow into plants from which new fruit grows. Does anyone know somebody who grows summer fruits in their garden?

Next, compare your selection of fruit by looking at and handling the complete fruit. How does size, shape, colour and texture vary? Encourage the children to describe the fruit by using words such as rough, smooth, prickly, sticky, soft, hard

and so on. Do they know the names of all the fruit? Which is the biggest and which is the smallest? Now ask the children to smell the outside of the fruit. Can they tell what it is just by its smell?

Having had a thorough examination of the outside of the fruit, help the children to cut the fruit in half both vertically and horizontally. Before you cut into the fruit ask the children to guess what the inside will be like. Will it be the same colour as the outside? Will the texture be the same? What colour and size will the stone/seeds be? Will the fruit smell different? The children should be in for a few surprises, especially if you include a few fruits such as water melon, kiwi fruit or passion fruit. Compare both cross-sections of fruit. What can they see in one which they can't see in the other?

Having looked carefully, felt and smelled the variety of fruit, finally, let the children taste some of it. Do they like the taste?

Discussion

Were you surprised by any of your discoveries about the fruit? Which were the biggest/smallest seeds you saw? Which seeds can you eat? Which fruit was your favourite?

Follow-up activities

✧ Peel some of the fruit and compare the skin. Look at the thick skin on melons and compare it with the very thin skin on peaches and nectarines.
✧ Compare seeds and stones of different fruits looking particularly at texture. Plant some and watch them grow — slowly!

FRUIT PRINTING

Objective

Art – To create a summer fruit wall hanging using potato printing techniques.

Group size

Six children.

What you need

Several potatoes, a peach, a cherry and a strawberry, yellow, white, red, black and blue poster paint, shallow trays, cloths, white sheeting or disposable tablecloth, sticky tape, blunt knives, teaspoons, modelling tools, pencils.

Preparation

Cut the fruit carefully in half, horizontally for the peach and cherry and vertically for the strawberry. Remove the stones. Cut several potatoes in half, some vertically and some horizontally. Cover tables with newspaper or PVC covering.

What to do

Examine the cut fruit together and help the children to create the shapes in the halved potatoes, hollowing out stone holes with blunt knives, teaspoons or modelling tools. Re-create the strawberry shape by cutting this shape on to a halved potato with a blunt knife. Add 'seeds' by pushing holes into the strawberry shape with a pencil point.

Help the children to mix up some thin poster paint in peach, dark purple and red. Place a little of this in the shallow trays, using one tray for each colour. Spread out the printing material and fix tightly to the table using sticky tape.

Assign two children to each tray and give them a piece of the relevant 'fruit' – 'peaches' for the peach paint, 'cherries' for the purple and 'strawberries' for the red. Encourage them to dip their 'fruit' in the paint and make prints on the material by pressing down firmly but gently and lifting the 'fruit' straight up again without twisting it. One dip in the paint should be enough for several prints.

After a little while, move the children around so that there is a mixture of fruit prints in any one place on the material. Encourage the children to try to achieve a mixture of colours and prints in the final piece of work. Use the printed sheet as a backdrop for a summer display.

Discussion

What happens if the paint is too runny / too thick? What happens if you move the 'fruit' as you are trying to make a print? Why can't we use the actual fruit to make prints? Summer fruits are soft and juicy and would disintegrate very quickly.

Follow-up activities

✧ Make patterns using seeds and stones from summer fruits such as melon seeds.
✧ Make a collage 'summer pudding' using strawberries, currants, cherries and so on cut from magazines. Alternatively, cut fruit shapes from red shades of paper, card or material.

THEMES
for early years

PICK YOUR OWN

Objective

Geography – To learn about fruit farms.

Group size

Whole group.

What you need

Books about fruit farming, pictures of soft fruit, some examples of soft fruit (optional), punnets and paper bags, wellington boots, weighing scales, toy money.

Preparation

Gather the children into a large circle around you, placing the books, pictures and props in the middle of the floor.

What to do

Start with a general discussion about how fruit grows. Can the children give you some examples of fruit which grows on trees, bushes or on the ground? Point out the differences between soft and hard fruits. Explain that farms which grow large quantities of fruit are called fruit farms and often people can go to these farms in the summer to pick their own soft fruit. Have any of the children ever done that? Ask any children who have to share their experiences with the other children, concentrating particularly on the large number of bushes and trees and how they are laid out so that people can walk between them.

If none of the children (or adults) has any experiences to relate, demonstrate what happens by asking various children to use the props to act out 'picking' the different fruit. First, tell them to put on wellington boots, so that their shoes don't get muddy in the fields. Then, tell them to imagine that they are picking fruit. Tell them a little about each type of fruit. Blackcurrants, for example, grow in strings hanging between the leaves of the bush and need to be found before they are gently stripped from the branches. Raspberries grow up supports and must be picked individually and very gently to prevent them being squashed. They also hide underneath leaves and need to be searched

for. Strawberries grow on the ground and you need to bend down low to pick them from the plant. They should be picked very gently and, if possible, with the green hull still attached to the fruit.

Let the children pretend to put the picked fruit carefully in the punnets or bags and then the farmer (another child) can weigh them on the scales and ask for the money.

Discussion

What do all plants need to grow well? How do we know when fruit is ripe? How will it change? How does the farmer keep the plants tidy?

Follow-up activities

✧ Make a fruit farm using modelling clay. Place 'fruit bushes' in rows with spaces in between.
✧ Talk about the need to water and spray fruit to keep it in good condition. Explain what organic produce is.
✧ Recite the poem 'Watch the wheat grow' on page 73.

PRESERVE IT!

Objective

History – To understand how food was kept palatable without refrigeration.

Group size

Whole group.

What you need

Books and pictures about housing and living in the past, salt, sugar and a selection of spices and herbs, both fresh and dried.

Preparation

Gather the children around you in a big circle and have all the books and props within easy reach.

What to do

Talk about hot days in the summer. What do we have to do with fresh food on these hot days? Demonstrate the need for refrigeration by leaving some fresh, soft fruit out in a warm room during hot weather and watching it deteriorate and go mouldy. (Don't let the children touch the mouldy fruit and dispose of it carefully.)

Explain that many years ago, before fridges and freezers were invented, people had to preserve their food in different ways.

Nowadays, we eat lots of fresh food, but long ago, it was unusual to eat completely fresh food.

Meat was preserved for many months, not by freezing it, but by salting it. Look at the salt and tell the children that although nowadays salt is very cheap and readily available, in the past it was highly sought after and extremely expensive. The salt prevented meat from decaying but it also removed much of the flavour so herbs and spices were used in order to make the food interesting and tasty to eat. Let the children smell the herbs and decide which they like.

Fish was preserved in a similar way, using salt, or by drying or smoking.

Sugar was widely used as a preservative as well and many fruits were boiled in syrup in order to prolong their life. Other food could be pickled in spices, herbs and vinegar.

Discussion

What do the children think it was like eating food prepared in this way? What must it have been like working in an old kitchen? Would it have been easy to prepare food quickly? Talk about larders with cold, slate slabs instead of fridges and freezers.

Follow-up activities

✧ Compare the smell of fresh and dried herbs. Do they smell different? Can the dried herbs be used for flavouring food? Discuss other dried food, such as Italian sun-dried tomatoes and dried meat – biltong – in southern Africa.

✧ Let the children cut out pictures of food which would nowadays be kept in a fridge or a freezer. Help them to stick these onto a giant fridge and freezer drawn on white card.

BARBECUE

Objective

English – To encourage speaking, listening and writing when designing an invitation to a summer barbecue.

Group size

Whole group.

What you need

Thin card in different colours, felt-tipped pens, pencils, crayons, sticky paper, collage pieces, glue, scissors.

Preparation

Spread out the paper, card and writing materials on the tables. Make sure that there is plenty of room for each child to work independently on their own invitation designs.

What to do

Have a general discussion about different types of parties, the reasons why people might have them and the different times of the year in which they are held. People have barbecues in the summer because the weather tends to be warmer and drier and it is pleasant to eat outside at this time of year. Do all the children know what happens at a barbecue? If not, encourage careful listening to and questioning of those who do.

Explain that you want the children to imagine that they are holding a summer barbecue for their friends. They will have to decide when and where the party will be held, who will be invited, what barbecue food will be eaten and whether the guests will need to wear fancy dress. Encourage open discussion, drawing out the less verbal among your group as well as letting the more extrovert have their say. Make sure that all aspects of the party are covered. Having allowed plenty of discussion, you may need to intervene in order to draw this to a conclusion.

Now turn the children's attention to the actual invitation. What size should it be? What colour card will you use? Encourage the children to think about who they are sending the invitation to and therefore, who it should appeal to. Should there be illustrations on it? What sort? What should the invitation say?

Write the words for the invitation on the board so they can be copied, such as 'Barbecue, Monday, Peter's House, Fancy Dress.' Then let the children design and decorate their own invitations around these guidelines.

Discussion

What sort of food can be barbecued? Could you cook this sort of food on your own? Why not? How does a summer barbecue differ from a picnic outside? Would you have a barbecue in the winter? Why not?

Follow-up activities

✧ Write a reply to the barbecue invitation.
✧ Make a list of food that needs to be bought or made for the barbecue.
✧ Look at recipe books for special barbecue food and note the instructive writing style.
✧ Ask the children to predict what would happen at the barbecue if it rained.

CHAPTER 5
SUMMER CLOTHES

This look at summer clothes includes finding out about changes in swimwear over the years, the need to keep cool in the heat, the properties of various materials and all about cotton. Patterns, shapes and sizes are all investigated and the children will dress a cut-out doll in summer clothes.

SWIMWEAR

Objective

History – To understand how the design of swimwear has changed over the years.

Group size

Whole group.

What you need

Books about costume including beachwear over the years (see page 96), with plenty of large illustrations, white card, felt-tipped pens, the photocopiable sheet on page 93, scissors.

Preparation

Ask the children to bring in their own swimwear from home to show to the rest of the group. Copy the photocopiable sheet and give one copy to each child in the group.

What to do

Start by talking about how, in the summer, we like to spend time swimming. Explain that the children are going to make a timeline, showing how swimwear has changed over the years. Let the children show and describe their swimsuits, trunks or bikinis to the other children. Most will be made of stretchy material which clings to the body. Have swimsuits always been like this?

Hand out and examine the photocopiable sheet together and guess which is the oldest of the designs for both men and women. Looking at the books and illustrations, going back in time, note the 'tennis skirt', the 'loose trouser and jacket' and the 'bathing dress' for ladies; the belted, woollen

trunks, bathing drawers and one-piece, striped suits for men. Encourage discussion about the different materials used and how these would have felt. The wool was uncomfortable and very heavy when wet, cotton did not stretch and the large quantities of material used in the loose dresses made them very awkward to swim in. Ladies wore ugly rubber swimming caps to keep their hair tidy and before these, bathers often swam in hats or bonnets.

Having talked about the various designs, invite the children to cut out and stick the swimwear in order along a card timeline, ending with a display of their own swimwear at the most recent end of the line.

Discussion

Why do you think swimwear used to be so different? Why were materials like wool used, not nylon and Lycra? Relate swimwear to other summer clothes worn in the past (see 'Sun and shade' on page 14 in Chapter 1).

Follow-up activities

✧ In a large bowl of water, compare the weight of wet wool and wet Lycra. Discuss the differences.
✧ Try 'sinking' a large piece of cotton sheeting in water. Air pockets will form and the material will billow out. Relate this to early bathing dresses.
✧ Say together the action rhyme 'Ready for the beach' on page 74.

IN THE HEAT

• •

Objective

RE – To learn about clothing worn in parts of the world where it is always hot.

Group size

Whole group.

What you need

Books about hot countries, with illustrations of the types of clothes worn there, long lengths of various thin materials, examples of 'hot' clothing such as Indian saris and dhotis, North African kaftans and galabias or Indonesian sarongs (optional).

Preparation

Gather the children together in a circle around you and spread out any examples of clothing on tables nearby.

What to do

Talk about how, in the summer months, the weather can be very hot. Discuss how, when we have a spell of hot weather in this country, we wear less clothes and choose ones made out of lighter material. In countries where it is always hot, some people wear clothes which are especially designed for the heat.

Encourage children with direct experience to share their knowledge with others in the group and throughout the discussion, be sensitive to the religious reasons for certain types of dress. Examine the examples of clothing you have or look at pictures in books to find common features. What are the clothes made of? Are they loose or tight-fitting? Do any cover the head as well? What colour are they? Develop a discussion about why these particular features are good in the constant heat of these countries.

Asking the children to imagine themselves on a very hot, sticky day will help. On such a day, tight, heavy, thick clothing is uncomfortable and loose, light, thin material is needed.

Now let the children try on some of the clothing if you have managed to borrow any or give them lengths of material to wrap around themselves. Sun hats keep their heads cool as do the hoods, head-dresses and headscarves worn with this special clothing. Dark colours absorb the heat, making the wearer even warmer and therefore, clothes designed for hot climates tend to be white or pale colours.

Discussion

Who has been to a hot country such as India or Africa? How does the hot weather affect the way the country looks? Do people do things in a different way because it is so hot?

Follow-up activities

✧ Help the children to create a cool garment by taking a square of light material, cutting a hole in the middle big enough for their head and slipping it on. Does it feel nice and cool to wear this on a very hot day?

✧ Sing the song 'In the heat' on page 84.

TOPS AND BOTTOMS

Objective

Art – To design co-ordinating clothes.

Group size

Four children.

What you need

Large sheets of sugar paper, pencils, crayons, brushes, poster paint, several patterned T-shirts and shorts, magazines or mail order catalogues containing pictures of children in T-shirts and shorts.

Preparation

Draw a large T-shirt and a pair of shorts on each piece of sugar paper to provide one for each child. Put the paint, brushes, pencils and crayons on the tables leaving plenty of space for the children to make their designs.

What to do

Talk to the children about summer clothes being bright and light weight. Do you enjoy wearing them? Say that T-shirts and shorts form part of the 'uniform' of summer for young children. Explain that they are going to design their own T-shirt and shorts to go well together, explaining that another word for this is to co-ordinate.

Demonstrate what you mean by showing the children some pictures in the magazines or catalogues where children are wearing tops and bottoms. Point out that if a child is wearing a patterned T-shirt he or she has plain shorts or ones with edging or a small pattern to match the top and vice versa. Use real clothes to demonstrate that if both are heavily patterned or the colours are too varied the effect is not so attractive.

Encourage the children to think about their own designs before they start to draw or paint them. Let them consider whether to use stripes, flowers, zigzags, checks, dots, animals, birds, film characters or some other design. Will their design be on the 'top' or on the 'bottom'? Having decided on the patterns and colours let the children use the materials to paint on the T-shirt and shorts shapes.

Help them to cut out the final versions, pin them in their pairs and display them all on a washing line along a wall of your room.

Discussion

If you use a red and yellow pattern on the T-shirt what would be a suitable colour for the shorts? How can you add a small amount of the same colour onto the other half of the outfit without creating a conflicting pattern? (Piping, collar, sleeve edging for example.)

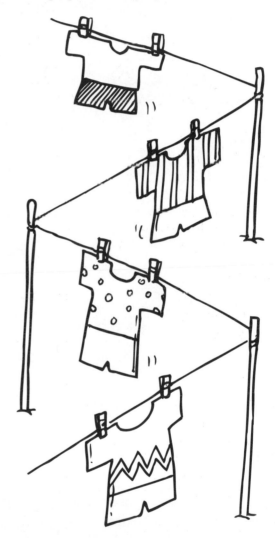

Follow-up activities

✧ Create a design using different shades of the same colour.
✧ Try creating a design using just letters and numbers.
✧ Make a symmetrical design by folding the T-shirt and shorts in half before making the pattern. Paint the design on one half and then fold over to replicate the pattern on the other side.

KEEPING COOL

Objective

Science – To look at the properties of various materials used for clothing.

Group size

Six children.

What you need

Two woollen jumpers, two cotton T-shirts and two waterproof nylon aprons, a very hot day!

Preparation

Sit around a table with all the different clothes within easy reach.

What to do

Talk about the importance of wearing the right clothes in order to keep cool on very hot summer days. In hot weather, your body is very hot and you will feel very sweaty and uncomfortable if you wear clothes which do not allow the heat to pass through them. However, if you wear clothes which allow your body heat to escape, you will feel cool and comfortable.

Explain to the children that they are going to try on various clothes in order to find out which materials are the nicest to wear in very hot weather. Ask for volunteers to try on the various items of clothing. After no longer than a couple of minutes,

just long enough for children to begin to feel uncomfortable, ask the children to report back on how they are feeling in their clothes.

Start with the wool; this will soon feel very hot and itchy. Children will start to sweat as the wool is a very compact material, very thick and heavy, and won't allow any heat to escape. The cotton should feel cool, light and comfortable as body heat can penetrate though it – it 'breathes'. Lastly, the waterproof, nylon apron will quickly feel very hot and sticky as body heat has no means of escaping through the material. Children will build up heat inside the apron, causing dampness and discomfort.

Let the children put the materials in order of suitability and comfort for hot days, perhaps cotton, wool and lastly, waterproof nylon.

Discussion

Where do wool, cotton and nylon come from? (See '100% cotton' on page 47.) Talk about the different sources of materials – animal, plant and manufactured fibres. Which of the fabrics lets heat pass through it to cool the body down?

Follow-up activities.

✧ Talk about how we like to keep cool in bed on hot summer nights by replacing woollen blankets with cotton sheets.
✧ Make a collection of summer clothing and examine the labels. See how many contain cotton.
✧ Sort a selection of fabric pieces into 'summer' and 'winter' materials.
✧ Recite the poem 'Cover up' on page 68.

100% COTTON

Objective

Geography – To understand how cotton grows and is harvested.

Group size

Whole group.

What you need

Books about cotton (see page 96), cotton wool balls, pads and thread, cotton clothes, paint, brushes, glue, card, blue backing paper.

Preparation

Spread out the books, cotton articles and clothes and gather the children together in a circle around you. Put the paint, brushes, glue and card on a separate table.

What to do

Referring back to 'Keeping cool' on page 46, ask the children where they think cotton to make cool clothes comes from. If anyone knows, let them contribute all they can before expanding in more detail yourself. Show the children the books and explain simply where cotton grows, how the plants develop and how the cotton fibre is collected, having been separated from the seeds in the seed pod or 'boll'.

Explain that the children are going to make a sequence display all about cotton, showing all the stages together with a collection of end products

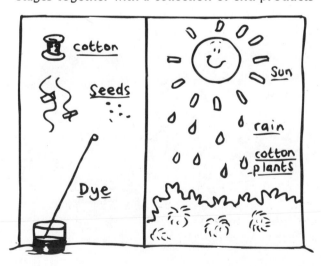

made from cleaned, dyed fibre which has been spun into thread.

Pin up a blue background (either paper or cloth) for the first half of the display, add a bright sun, raindrops (cotton plants grow where it is hot and wet), flowering cotton plants and plants with 'bolls' which have burst – add cotton wool balls to the painted plants to create this effect. In the second half, the children could paint separated fibres and seeds and display these leading to painted pots of dye, finishing with actual spools of thread in different colours along with several examples of cotton material, some made into clothes or furnishing fabrics.

Discussion

What has to be done to the cotton from the plant before it can be made into thread? Have you seen the fleece shorn from a sheep? What has to be done to this wool to clean and untangle it before it can be spun into yarn? Note the similarities.

Follow-up activities

✧ Talk about other plants which produce fibres – linen for clothes, hemp for sacks and rope, jute for string and mats and sisal for ropes. Examine some examples together.
✧ Compare different kinds of cotton cloth and thread – muslin, towelling, denim, lace, string, embroidery thread, canvas and tulle. Notice how they are all made from the same plant, but they all feel very different.

OPPOSITES

. . . .

Objective

English – To understand the meaning of opposite.

Group size

Whole group, split into three smaller groups.

What you need

A selection of summer and winter clothing, in both child and adult sizes.

Preparation

Spread out all the clothing in any order on child-sized tables.

What to do

Let the children sort through the clothing, noting that some of it will be suitable for winter wear and some for summer. Explain that summer clothes tend to be short-sleeved, made of thin material and light in colour. In contrast, winter clothes are thick, dark and long-sleeved. When something is totally different in this way, we say that it is the opposite. Identify three pairs of opposite words for the children such as: dark/light, thick/thin, long/short.

Now, ask the first group of children to sort the clothes into those for summer and those for winter. By examining the two piles, ask them what pairs of opposites they can come up with. For example, all winter clothes will be 'warm' – the opposite being 'cool' in the summer pile. Other pairs could include high/low (neckline), open/closed (shoes and sandals), tight/loose (woolly hat and sun-hat), heavy/light (jumper and T-shirt).

The next group of children should sort the clothing again into adult and child sizes, regardless of the type of clothing. Examine again and think up more opposites for these two piles, such as large/small, wide/narrow, child-like/grown-up.

The last group of children should look just at the summer clothes, restricting their search for opposites to the type of pattern or lack of it on the clothing such as: patterned/plain, small/large (checks/dots), zigzag/straight (stripes) or open/closed (flowers).

Discussion

What 'opposites' do you encounter every day? Think about such things as hot and cold taps, on and off switches, being wet and dry. If you are hungry, what do you do in order to feel the opposite (full)?

Follow-up activities

✧ Play an action game which involves the children listening to instructions and doing the opposite, for instance – hold your hand 'up' – the children have to put their hand 'down' and so on.

✧ Tell a group story. Each child has to add more to the story, using the opposite word to the one just used. For example: the 'big' man lived in a 'small' house, his clothes were 'clean' but his house was 'dirty'.

WILL IT FIT?

Objective

Mathematics – To learn to estimate when considering size and shape.

Group size

Six children.

What you need

A range of summer clothing and shoes in both adult and child sizes, different sized dolls and teddies, together with some clothes for them.

Preparation

Give each child a mixture of clothing and a doll each if possible, or one shared between two. Ask them to sit in a circle around you.

What to do

Introduce the activity by holding up some of the clothing and reminding the children that summer clothes need to be light, cool and comfortable, like these items. Next, ask them to sort the clothes into adult, child and doll sizes, referring them back to opposites in size and shape – narrow/wide, large/small (see page 48). The children should be able to work out relatively easily that adult clothes will be too big/long/wide for them and doll's clothes will be too small/short/narrow. However, it may be more difficult for them to estimate whether their own clothes will fit a friend, an adult's clothes will fit a different adult or doll's clothes will fit another doll or teddy. This is when it becomes necessary to think about shape as well as overall size.

Turning to each child in turn, ask him/her to hold up an article from their pile of clothing. Who is this garment designed for? Will it fit a child, adult or doll? Will it fit every child/adult/doll? Remain sensitive to the children's feelings about their different weights and heights, while you encourage the children to look carefully at their friends, dolls and adults in the group, in order to decide whether items of clothing/shoes will fit them. They need to be precise about their answers, for example, 'this dress is the right length but it will be too wide for Clare' or 'this T-shirt is too tight and too short for Tom'. Encourage them to estimate by looking first. The children can then check their guesses by asking the children involved to actually try on the items of clothing.

Discussion

How accurate were your guesses? Was it easier to guess right lengths or widths? Was it difficult to guess correct shoe size?

Follow-up activities

✧ From a selection of belts – or use ribbons – ask children to pick out one which will fit around their own waists.
✧ Can they find a child's T-shirt to fit a large teddy?

MANNEQUINS

Objective

Design and Technology – To practise cutting and folding skills when making a mannequin doll.

Group size

Four children.

What you need

Photocopiable page 94, one for each child, scissors, sticky tape, modelling clay.

Preparation

Stick the photocopy of the 'doll' (enlarged to A3) onto card, copy the remainder of the sheet, same size, ready for use. Sit the children down at tables, with their photocopies and scissors. Allow them plenty of room to work independently.

What to do

Explain that the children are going to be cutting out their own dolls and clothes in order to create a doll dressed for a hot summer's day. Before examining the clothing on the sheet, ask the children what they might expect their doll to be wearing (summer dress/shorts and T-shirt, sun-hat). Children will feel a tremendous sense of achievement if they manage to cut out the various shapes for themselves, so encourage them to be independent, only offering help where this is absolutely necessary. You might however suggest that they cut roughly around each item of clothing before they try cutting out a more accurate shape.

Stress the importance of leaving the small white flaps intact as these will be used to fold the clothes over the body of the mannequin. Provide scissors that are sufficiently sharp, as blunt scissors which do not cut properly are extremely frustrating; ensure safety by demonstrating how to handle sharp things properly. Make sure that the children hold the scissors correctly so that the blades cut through the paper and card cleanly.

When they have cut out all the various pieces of clothing, help them to assemble the doll. Stand the 'doll' in a lump of modelling clay, take a piece of clothing and show children how to fold the tabs

backwards so that they fit tightly around the body of the doll when the clothes are placed in the right position. Let the children finish 'dressing' the dolls in this way.

Discussion

Why do we have to cut the dolls out of card when the clothes can be paper? What could we use to keep the clothes permanently in place on the dolls? (Sticky tape.)

Follow-up activities

✧ Draw faces on the mannequin dolls, glue on wool hair and colour the clothes.
✧ Cut out and decorate some beach balls and ice-creams for the children to use with their dolls.
✧ Encourage children to give their dolls names and play with them once the clothes are taped in position.

CHAPTER 6
HOLIDAYS

Why do we have holidays? Where do we go? In these activities the children think about preparing for holidays, deciding what to take, packing up and travelling as well as learning about the difficulties of travel in the past.

A WELL-EARNED REST!

Objective

RE – To realize the importance of building relationships.

Group size

Whole group.

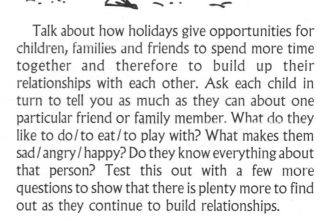

What you need

Photographs of friends and families (provided by the children), a large display board, Blu-Tack.

Preparation

Send a note home to parents asking children to bring in photographs of family and friends, particularly those taken on holiday. Sit all the children in a big circle with their photographs. Set up the display board close to you so that all the children can see.

What to do

Start by explaining that the summer is a time when many people try to take a holiday, taking time away from their work or learning to have a restful time with family and friends. Being sensitive to and aware of the different family situations which may arise, ask each child in turn to tell the group about their photographs, putting them up on the board so that everyone can see.

Encourage the children to explain who is in their pictures, where the pictures were taken and what the people were doing at the time. Were they, for instance, away on holiday, on a day out, or staying with friends or relatives? What do the children like to do with their friends? Talk about the games they enjoy playing together and spending the day at each other's houses.

Talk about how holidays give opportunities for children, families and friends to spend more time together and therefore to build up their relationships with each other. Ask each child in turn to tell you as much as they can about one particular friend or family member. What do they like to do/to eat/to play with? What makes them sad/angry/happy? Do they know everything about that person? Test this out with a few more questions to show that there is plenty more to find out as they continue to build relationships.

Discussion

How would people feel if they had no friends? What can you do to ensure that everyone does have friends? What do the children and family members do to relax? Talk about reading, watching TV, listening to music and so on.

Follow-up activities

✧ Take the role of a new member joining your group for the first time. Ask the children how this new member might feel. How can the others help him/her?
✧ Ask the children to give you a verbal list of all the things that are done for them during the day. Invite them to think about cooking, washing, cleaning, shopping and so on. How can they help?

I TOOK WITH ME...

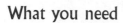

Objective

English — To encourage careful listening and accurate recall.

Group size

Whole group.

What you need

A quiet, attentive group, a selection of summer items such as sunscreen, T-shirt, sunglasses, sun-hat and so on.

Preparation

The group can sit on the floor or at tables. Encourage silence by asking them to be very quiet and listen carefully. What can they hear?

What to do

Having established relative silence, explain that you are going to play a memory game which requires the children to listen very carefully if they are going to be able to play it successfully.

Ask the children to imagine that they are going on holiday in the summer. Decide between you where you are going on the trip and ask the children to suggest the type of things they might take with them when they pack their suitcases. Start the game with one child saying 'I took with me (for example) my swimming trunks'. Continue the game with each child in turn repeating what has been said and then adding another item. For example, the third child in the group might say 'I took with me my swimming trunks, my sun-hat and my sunscreen'. Encourage maximum thought and effort by challenging: Who can remember the most items? If a child is having difficulty remembering, try not to offer help too quickly, but allow the child plenty of time to think and, if necessary let other children help out.

After a while, vary the game by putting the selection of summer items in a pile in the middle of your group, and asking children to hold items up silently after they have said the words 'I took with me...'. The game now involves careful watching rather than listening.

Discussion

Which game did you find easier? Did it help having the actual articles to look at? If there was noise in the group as you were trying to remember, did that make it more difficult?

Follow-up activities

✧ Make up a sentence involving three children taking three different kinds of luggage on their holiday (a suitcase, a bag and a rucksack). Can the children remember who takes what?
✧ Tell a short story about a summer holiday. Can the children remember characters, events and outcomes?

THIS IS THE WAY...

Objective

PE/Drama — To convey meaning through mime.

Group size

Whole group.

What you need

A large space in which the children can move around freely, a selection of travel brochures.

Preparation

Ask the children to find a space and sit down in it. They should not be able to touch anyone.

What to do

Encourage the children to think about all the things that need to happen before we go off on our summer holidays or day trips. Well before the holiday they may remember grown-ups and perhaps themselves, looking at travel brochures and discussing together in order to decide where they should go. Show the brochures to any children who may not have seen them before. Remind the children that, having decided where the holiday is going to be, they have to book and pay for it, perhaps over the telephone or by visiting a travel agent. Nearer the departure date, they will need to pack suitcases with everything they want to take with them. On the day, they wave goodbye as they get on the train, plane, bus, coach or in the car.

Explain that they are going to act out, to an imaginary audience, several of these things to the tune of 'Here we go Round the Mulberry Bush'. Start with 'This is the way we decide where to go', continuing with 'This is the way we book the holiday' and 'This is the way we pack what we need' and ending with 'This is the way we set off on holiday'. Offer the children a general framework and then allow them freedom to develop individual actions to represent the activities.

Discussion

Where is your favourite place to visit when on holiday or when making day trips? Who has been on a plane/a train/a coach? Do you help your mum/dad decide what things to take on holiday?

Follow-up activities

✧ Divide the children into three groups and ask each group to pretend they are either planes, trains or cars.
✧ Sing the song 'Pack my suitcase' on page 87.
✧ Say together the action poem, 'Ready for the beach' on page 74 before singing 'By the sea' on page 87 to the same traditional tune of 'Here we go Round the Mulberry Bush'.
✧ Let the children mime some of the things people might do on holiday — swim in the sea, climb a mountain, pitch a tent, ride a horse and so on.

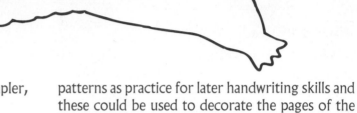

BESIDE THE SEA

Objectives

English — To practise handwriting skills by producing a class 'Big book'; to encourage observational and listening skills.

Group size

Whole group.

What you need

Pencils, wide-lined paper, white card, glue, stapler, coloured pencils, scissors, seaside pictures.

Preparation

Draw and cut out several large, seagull shapes from the card and staple these together to form the 'Big book'. Cut the lined paper into pieces which will fit onto the seagull shapes and give one piece of paper to each child.

What to do

Talk to your group about the seaside and what they might expect to see there. If some of them have no direct experience, show them as many pictures as possible and encourage other group members to share their knowledge with them.

Act as scribe during the discussion, making a list of relevant words, such as shells, donkeys, boats, beach balls, sandcastles, ice-cream and so on. As well as the more usual sights, try to get the children to think about less obvious things such as seaweed, sandhoppers, crabs and waves. Next, think about what they might hear. This will obviously depend on the specific seaside environment and you may need to have a further discussion to stimulate ideas. Don't forget the noises and excitement of funfairs and amusement arcades, children laughing and playing, bandstands, fish and chip sellers and so on. Try to generate memories of some of the gentler sounds too, such as waves breaking on the shore, the crunch of shingle underfoot, seagulls crying, sails flapping and wind blowing through the dunes.

Finally, help each child to write a piece for the 'Big book' beginning 'I can see...'/'I can hear...'. Younger children could make or follow wave patterns as practice for later handwriting skills and these could be used to decorate the pages of the 'Big book'.

Discussion

When do people usually go to the seaside? Why? Are all 'seasides' the same? Is the beach always sandy? Are there always rocks on the shore? Are there always lots of people? Talk about other environments such as muddy estuaries, barren cliffs, tiny harbours and busy ports.

Follow-up activities

✧ Ask the children to illustrate the 'Big book' either by drawing pictures or by cutting pictures from magazines to fit the seagull shapes.
✧ Complete the photocopy on page 95.
✧ Look at pictures of various sea birds. How many have the children seen?
✧ Sing the song 'Sun and sand' on page 85 and say the rhymes 'Five wobbly jelly fish', page 76, 'Seaside song', page 74 and 'What am I?', page 71.

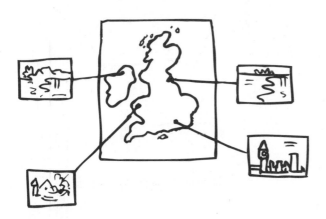

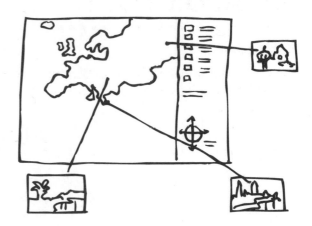

WHERE HAVE YOU BEEN?

• •

Objective

Geography — To begin to understand maps.

Group size

Whole group.

What you need

A large map of the United Kingdom and of the world, a display board, postcards showing different geographical features (the seaside, hills and mountains, towns and the countryside), wool, drawing pins.

Preparation

Send a letter home to parents, asking children to bring in postcards showing summer holiday destinations. Fix the maps to the display board and sit the children where they can all see.

What to do

Start by looking together at the maps. Explain that the children are going to be finding out how the places they have visited are shown on a map. Locate the area where your group live and describe how it looks on the map — probably a greyish dot if an urban area and green or brown if countryside.

On both maps there will be a large area of both green and blue. Explain to the children that the land is shown as green and the sea as blue. When land has sea all the way around it, that piece of land is called an island. The United Kingdom is made up of several islands. Point these out to the children.

Now ask any children with seaside pictures to hold them up. Invite them to describe the blue sea and sandy beach/rocky shore. Where do they think these areas might be on the map? (Emphasize seaside.) Ask a child to point to a suitable area on the map. Now explain that there are many seaside areas in the world and you need to find the correct place for each child's postcard. Join it to the relevant place on the maps with wool.

Look at postcards of towns, countryside, hills and mountains. All these areas are land. Will they all look the same on the map? Explain that towns and cities are generally shown as greyish dots, low land is shown green whereas higher land is brownish-yellow. Encourage children to find suitable places for their postcards, again rearranging them into the correct positions afterwards.

Discussion

Can you show me an area of the world which has lots of mountains? Find the United Kingdom on the map. The UK is a small island, can you find Australia — a very big island?

Follow-up activities

✧ Collect various pictures showing geographical features and four boxes coloured green, brown, grey and blue. Ask the children to sort the pictures into the correctly coloured box according to the colouring used on maps.

✧ Looking in more detail at the map, ask the children what they think the thin blue lines and patches of blue in the middle of green land might possibly be.

LET'S KEEP BUSY!

Objective

History — To understand the difficulty of early travel.

Group size

Whole group.

What you need

Pictures of, and books about old and new forms of transport, a large space.

Preparation

Sit the children down and spread out the pictures and books within easy reach.

What to do

Summer is traditionally a time for taking holidays away from home. This inevitably involves travelling — by bus, coach, car, train, boat or plane. Ask who has been on any of these forms of transport. Choose children to be a plane pilot, a train driver, a boat captain and a coach driver.

Divide the other children up into groups and let them be transported from A to B by their 'drivers'. Suggest actions, such as spreading their arms for the plane, walking unsteadily for the boat, bouncing up and down for the coach and leaning to one side and then the other for the train.

Explain that about 100 years ago, it was not so easy for people to get about. Although travelling by rail and by boat was reasonably fast, comfortable and cheap, going by road was very difficult. There were very few cars, they weren't able to go very fast and people had to have lots of money to be able to buy them. Choose one child to be the garage owner and two more to be customers. One child hands over lots of pretend money and goes off very slowly in his car. The other child is sent away empty-handed having failed to produce enough money.

Travel by aeroplane was not possible at that time, so people didn't travel nearly as much as they do now. Instead, they used to stay close to home, playing outside, going for walks and picnics, riding bicycles and so on.

Discussion

When looking at the pictures of old and new transport, discuss how trains and boats have changed. Look at the differences in design and discuss how they used to be driven by steam, not diesel engines. What was used to heat the water and turn it into steam? Who has seen coal? What does it look like?

Follow-up activities

✧ Try to borrow some accurate models of old transport or arrange a visit to a transport museum.
✧ Talk about the changes in indoor entertainment over the years, from song recitals around the piano to computer games.
✧ Sing the songs 'Pot-pourri' and 'Playing out' on page 83.
✧ Say together the action rhyme 'Sunshine and shadows' on page 69.

CLEVER PACKING!

Objective

Mathematics – To develop spatial awareness.

Group size

Four children.

What you need

A small suitcase, several boxes and packages of different shapes, sizes and colours to represent various items of luggage, enough to fill the suitcase comfortably.

Preparation

Spread out all the items and the suitcase on a table near the children.

What to do

Start by establishing that everybody knows the shape of a rectangle and a square. Now ask the children to imagine that they are packing to go away on their summer holiday. They will be packing empty boxes and packages instead of actual luggage. Do they do their own packing or do adults do it for them? Explain that with a little bit of practice, they could become quite good at doing this for themselves.

Show them the suitcase and the various items to be packed and then set the challenge. They have to try to pack all the items in the suitcase so that the lid can be easily closed and nothing gets squashed. Encourage experimentation to begin with. Make sure the children look at shape as well as size. If help is needed, ask them to look at the length and width of the suitcase. Help them to find an item which is as long or as wide as this and put this in first. Then invite them to build on this 'puzzle' by slotting in other items around these, gradually filling the case.

If they end up with no more room and spaces around pieces of luggage, they will need to start again and see if they can use the space more efficiently. Use as much positional language as possible, for example, 'the small yellow box is on top of/next to the big blue one'.

Discussion

What shapes have we got? (Try to have a mixture of different sized squares and rectangles.) If we put two rectangles side by side, what shape have we made? If we put two squares side by side, what shape have we made? How does this help us?

Follow-up activities

✧ Introduce a few triangular items as well to make the 'puzzle' a little more difficult.
✧ Give each child a piece of large-squared paper to represent a suitcase. Ask them to colour in sets of these squares to make rectangular and bigger square shapes and see how they fit together in their 'paper suitcase.'
✧ Try packing all the boxes and packages into a holdall of a similar size. Is this easier or more difficult? Why?
✧ Sing the song 'Pack my suitcase' on page 87.

HAND LUGGAGE

. . . .

Objective

Design and Technology – To make a small suitcase using a variety of techniques.

Group size

Four children.

What you need

A sturdy shoe box for each child, thick sticky tape, treasury tags, paper fasteners, thick string, rubber bands, a skewer (for adult use only).

Preparation

Spread out all the resources on tables within easy reach of the children.

What to do

In the summertime, when children go on holiday, they often need a small case, known as hand luggage, in which to carry the items they will need during their journey such as a teddy, a snack, a drink, a book and so on. Explain that the children are going to make a piece of hand luggage using the materials which you have put on the tables. Ask the children to think about what the suitcase will need. (It must have a hinged lid, a catch of some sort and a handle for carrying it.)

The shoebox is going to be the body and lid of the case. Ask for suggestions for attaching the lid to the body. Tape could be used but will not work if extended beyond the ends of the lid. Short treasury tags could also be used, inserting ends into holes on the body and the lid. (Adults will need to pierce the holes with a skewer.)

Having made the bulk of the case, encourage the children to add a catch and handle. Paper fasteners inserted into the lid and the body provide 'anchors' for a rubber band catch. Wind the band several times around the paper fastener on the lid before separating its 'arms' and pressing down firmly. Leave the other end free to slip around the fastener on the body when the case is closed.

Make a handle to attach to the case from the string. Pierce two holes in the body of the case, feed the string through and tie a knot at each end.

Discussion

Why shouldn't children use the skewer? Could they use thin sticky tape to attach the lid? If the string handle pulls out of the case, what could they put on the ends of the string to stop that happening?

Follow-up activities

✧ Make a book to take away on holiday. Use several sheets of paper and encourage children to think of different ways they could attach the pages together.
✧ Ask the children to pretend that they have forgotten their purse. What junk material could they use to keep their pennies in? (Sweet tubes, film canisters.)

CHAPTER 7
DISPLAYS

Ideas for complete displays, based around some of the activities earlier in the book are detailed in this chapter. Further suggestions for display ideas are included within the activity chapters.

Involve the children in the preparation of every display you put up, although the final assembly will probably have to be done by you. Let them paint, cut out, stick, bring things from home and offer ideas and suggestions. Simply worded, large-lettered, lower case labels can add greatly to the impact of a display. Achieve simple 3D effects by gently bending items in the display or padding them out with crumpled newspaper and stapling them slightly away from the board. This really brings the display to life and is well worth doing.

IN THE DESERT

What you need

A display board at child height, covered with yellow or cream lining paper, orange, yellow, red, brown and green poster paint, several sponges, brushes, pieces of material for a collage, shiny paper, tissue and packaging in yellows, gold and oranges, PVA glue, card, plastic plates, staple gun, black felt-tipped pen.

What to do

With the children's help, mix up several shades of 'sand' coloured poster paint. Use yellow paint as a base and add smaller quantities of orange, red and brown. Pour a small amount onto flat plates and provide one sponge for each shade. Having made sure that the children are wearing effective overalls and that the floor is suitably protected, ask two children at a time to sponge a background for the desert scene by dipping their sponges carefully into the paint and 'patting' the paper with it. Do not allow them to 'rub' or the result will not be as effective. For best results, change the colours the children are working with fairly regularly. Depending on the size of your display board, you may need to assist after a while.

Choose another group to make a hot sun. Draw a large circle on the card and let the children stick

collage pieces all over this, again mixing colours and textures as much as possible. Draw several cacti and snakes onto card and let the children paint these. Use various shades of green for the cacti, adding 'spines' with black felt-tipped pen. Let the children paint the snakes using their own patterns.

If your drawing skills are good enough, you could also draw camels and scorpions for the children to paint!

Finally, cut out the various items and assemble the display against the sponge-printed background. Place a few real cacti on a table in front of the display, together with a shallow sand tray in which children can feel the dry sand and play with toy desert animals. Remind the children not to touch the cacti.

Discussion

Encourage children to imagine themselves in this alien environment. What would they hear? (Very little probably — perhaps the hiss of a snake or the wind blowing sand around.) What would they feel? (The dry sand trickling through their toes, the heat of the sun, the scaly snake and the prickly cacti.)

The Sun is hot
like it or not
So do take care
make sure you wear..

If you drink a lot
you won't get too hot
Stay out a short time
and remember this rhyme!

THE SUMMER SUN

What you need

A display board backed in bright blue paper. Bright yellow or orange card, poster paint in lots of colours including red, yellow and orange, brushes, small sponge rollers, small articles for printing such as LEGO bricks, corks, blunt pencils, cotton reels, Unifix bricks, bottle tops and so on, shallow dishes, large drawings on card of a T-shirt, a pair of shorts, a legionnaire sun-hat, a pair of sunglasses, a bottle of sun cream, a glass of juice and a clock.

What to do

Write out the following rhyme in large lettering to fix to one side of the display:

> The sun is hot
> Like it or not
> So do take care
> Make sure you wear...

Now ask the children to create a glowing sun. Cut out a large circle of yellow card. Mix up several shades of yellow and orange paint and pour a little into each shallow dish. Let two children in turn dip the small objects into the paint and make prints all over the sun. When the sun is completely covered staple it to the middle of the blue 'sky'. Let other children make patterns on the T-shirts and shorts in any colours they wish, using the foam rollers. Another group of children could paint the other accessories. Fix the T-shirt, shorts, sun-hat, glasses and sun cream under the rhyme. Explain that when the sun is very hot, we can get very thirsty and we must drink plenty. It is also not a good idea to stay in the sun for too long. Say this rhyme together, write it out and add it to the display on the other side, together with the glass and clock:

> If you drink a lot
> You won't get too hot
> Stay out a short time and
> Remember this rhyme.

Ask the children to bring in some of the things they wear in the sun in order to make an interactive display. (Only use empty bottles of sun cream!) Put these in front of the wall display.

Discussion

Are there similarities between the items the children have brought from home? Look at the materials the clothes are made from. What do the different numbers on the sun cream bottles mean? Why are there long flaps on some of the sun-hats? How do sunglasses differ from ordinary glasses?

AT THE SEASIDE

What you need

A display board covered in dark green or dark blue lining paper, dark red, pink, green and brown material remnants, felt and tissue paper, bubble wrap and small polythene food bags (for adult use only), card, blue, silver and green shiny paper, scissors, stapler (for adult use only), sticky tape, PVA glue, pipe-cleaners, sand, shells and pebbles.

What to do

Help the children to make seaweed by showing them how to tear tissue paper into long, thin strips. They can also make it from the material remnants by tearing along an incision which you have made or by cutting felt into strips. Make the strips into effective seaweed on the display board by twisting these strips and stapling them into flowing shapes. Make crabs by scrunching up a sheet of brown or green tissue paper and attaching pipe-cleaner legs with sticky tape. Make jelly fish by blowing up polythene bags and taping on strips of bubble wrap for the tentacles. Draw several fish on the card and encourage children to add silver, blue and green scales which they have cut from the shiny paper before they cut out the whole fish.

Complete the display by weaving the various sea creatures in and out of the seaweed. In front of the wall display, put a small table covered with a thin layer of sand.

Encourage children to add the shells and pebbles to make this look like a beach. Add the summer mannequins from the activity 'Mannequins' on page 50.

Discussion

What other things have the children seen at the seaside? The wall display is showing the various things in the sea water, rather than on the beach or on the water. What else might they find in the water? Talk about prawns, lobsters, octopi, eels and so on.

What might they find on the beach? Talk here about hermit crabs, worms of various sorts, sandhoppers, mussels, cockles and all sorts of shells. What might we find on the water?

Can the children think of anything other than boats and ships of various kinds? (Sea birds, mooring and navigation buoys, floating wood, oil and rubbish — sadly!)

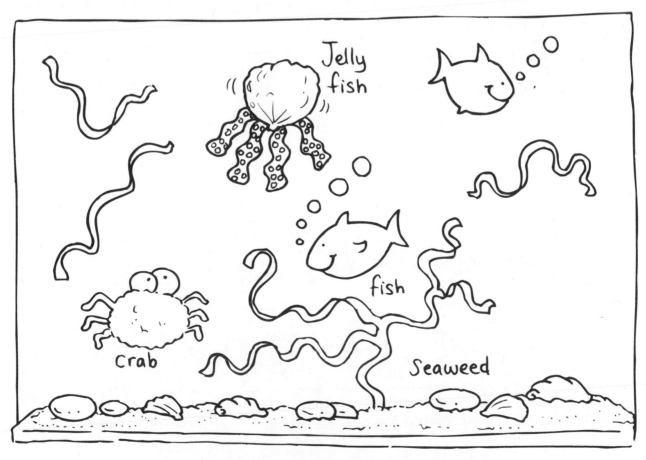

INSECT WORLD

What you need

A display board covered in bright green backing paper, coloured paper or card, Cellophane or tissue paper, scissors, PVA glue, a stapler (for adult use only), felt and material pieces, pipe-cleaners, pictures of sweet food such as fruit and cakes, dark green poster paint, adhesive tape, thick black felt-tipped pen, a paper plate.

What to do

Allow two children to scrumple up pieces of the material and dip them into dark green paint then to sponge patches of darker 'grass' onto the green backing paper. Draw some flower petals on the coloured card or paper and let the children cut these out, together with long, thin stems. Staple these straight onto the board, arranging the petals in a circle around the flower stem to make beautiful flowers. Let the children cut out and glue some of the sweet foods onto the paper plate before attaching it to the display.

Now make the insects. Cut a number of ovals from the card (choose the size according to the size of your display board) and invite the children to glue on material or felt in browny colours (bees),

yellow and black (wasps), red (ladybirds) and black (ants). Help them to add pipe-cleaner legs and feelers and Cellophane or tissue paper wings by cutting to size and taping these to the back of the card ovals. Add black 'ladybird' spots with the felt-tipped pen and cut small pieces of felt (food) for the ants to carry away. Invite the children to decorate butterfly shapes as they wish, painting thickly onto one half of the shape and transferring this pattern symmetrically to the other half by folding over and pressing down firmly. As before, add pipe-cleaner feelers.

Arrange all the insects as desired on the flowers, grass and plate before adding a few labels as suggested.

Put a table in front of the display on which you can put either a wormery (layers of different soils and sand in a narrow tank in which worms make tunnels) or a tank environment for snails, together with picture books about insects.

Discussion

Refer back to the activity 'Insect World' on page 16 and remind children about the various insects and how they behave. Encourage them to look regularly at the worms or snails. What are they doing? What have they eaten? Which insects in the display can fly? Can you name any other insects?

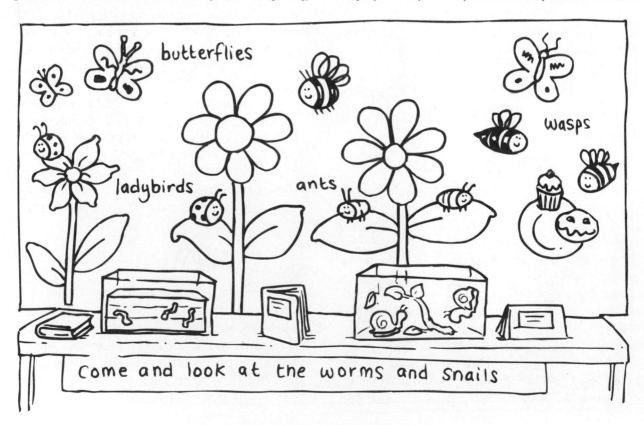

Come and look at the worms and snails

GIVE ME SUNSHINE

• •

What you need

A display board covered half with black paper and half with yellow paper, green, brown and yellow card, tissue paper in white and green, thick white string, stapler (for adult use only), paintbrush, PVA glue.

What to do

Referring back to the activity 'Give me Sunshine' on page 24, remind the children that plants need light in order to grow healthily. Point out the two different sides of the display board and explain that one is black in order to represent growth in dark conditions, while the other is yellow to represent a plant growing in the sunshine. The children are going to make the various parts of the plants, growing in both kinds of conditions.

Draw two pot shapes on the brown card and leaves on the yellow and green card and ask the children to carefully cut these out. Let them cut different lengths of thick string to resemble roots and help them to glue these downwards on the brown card pot. When the 'pots' are ready, staple one to each side of the display board. Ask the

children to tell you what colours the stems of the two plants would be. Hopefully, they will remember that the 'dark' plant will have a white stem and the 'light' plant, a green one. Show them how to twist long lengths of the tissue paper into thin stems and then staple these to the board, coming out of the pots. The 'dark' stem will be very long and spindly whereas the 'light' one will be thicker and shorter. Add leaves in green or yellow, according to growing conditions.

Finish the display by putting some real plants on a table in front of it, together with the important things which have made these plants grow healthily such as compost, water (display an empty watering can) and a large picture of a bright sun. Cover one of the plants with a large, black card cone so that the children can see how different a plant grown in the dark really looks.

Discussion

Ask the children to imagine how they would feel if they were always in the dark. Why do they think the 'dark' plants grow so long and spindly? (They are trying to reach the light.) Refer this spindly growth to trees growing in a thick forest. These trees grow very tall and thin as they try to reach the light above the forest.

CHAPTER 8
ASSEMBLIES

This chapter suggests ideas for assemblies or group sharing times on the theme of 'Summer' and includes activities, prayers and songs.

HOLIDAYS

In this assembly, children can draw on any experiences they may have had during a range of practical activities related to this topic. They should have begun to identify some of the key features of a typical holiday and explore the reasons why people may choose to travel far from home. This should help them to develop a future understanding of the place of pilgrimage in a range of different faith traditions.

Introduction

As the children enter the assembly area, play appropriate music such as 'Summer Holiday' by Cliff Richard or 'Holiday' by Madonna.

Show the children three small suitcases and explain that each one belongs to someone who has returned recently from a holiday. Invite members of the audience to come and open them and to show the contents of each one to the rest of the group. The items in each case should reflect a different type of holiday, such as a walking tour, a city break or a stay by the sea. Include appropriate articles of clothing and equipment, guidebooks postcards and souvenirs.

Encourage the children to suggest where each imaginary person may have been on holiday and ask them to offer some possible reasons why they may have chosen their respective destinations.

What to do

Inform the children that people who belong to different faith communities may go on a special kind of holiday called a pilgrimage.

Invite various children to come forward to talk about different pilgrimage destinations, such as Jerusalem, Canterbury, Lourdes or Makkah. Try to reflect the faith and traditions which are represented within your school or group and ask the children to tell everyone about each of the places selected – this should be prepared in advance. Use a large

map to show the location of each site and display pictures, posters, souvenirs and other artefacts.

Encourage the children to highlight what happens in each pilgrimage centre and encourage them to explore some of the reasons why people may visit these special places.

Reflection

Encourage the children to sit quietly and to close their eyes.

Play some peaceful background sounds, such as leaves rustling or the sea lapping on the shore (health food shops and garden centres often stock a range of suitable tapes and CDs).

Encourage the children to picture their own favourite special holiday destination, perhaps one they have already visited or one where they would like to go in the future. Ask them to imagine what they would do there, how they would feel and to consider why their particular place is special.

Prayer

Conclude the gathering by inviting those who wish to do so to listen to a short prayer about holidays or pilgrimages. This could perhaps be written by one of the children or selected from a suitable anthology.

Music

Continue playing some suitable recorded music or invite the children to sing an appropriate piece selected from this book.

THE SUN

This assembly offers children the opportunity to explore the importance of the sun as a source of light and warmth. They will be able to draw on experiences they may have had during other activities, particularly in science, geography and design technology.

The assembly will also lay down the foundations for an understanding of the way in which Christians use the sun as a symbol for God.

Introduction

Open the gathering with a recording of a song about the sun, such as 'Here Comes the Sun' by The Beatles.

Begin by inviting the children to share with one another some examples of the work that they have undertaken which links with this topic. They could show paintings, drawings, graphs and charts which illustrate the power of the sun and present or perform a selection of appropriate rhymes, poems, stories and songs.

Summarize this introduction by emphasizing that the sun is essential to life.

What to do

Inform the children that Christians sometimes use the sun as a symbol for God: this is because they believe that God is necessary to their lives.

Invite some children to show a large painted circle in reds, yellows and oranges to represent the sun and place it on a display board in the centre of the gathering.

Ask individual children to come forward one by one, with strips of appropriately coloured paper to represent the rays of the sun. Each strip should feature a word which could be used to describe the sun – powerful, strong, warm, comforting, glowing, light and so on. Place the strips on the display board around the central circle until the design is complete.

Encourage the children to consider how and why Christians might use the same words to describe God.

Reflection

Find a suitable OHP transparency of a glorious sunrise and display it on a screen. Play some peaceful, reflective music quietly in the background and slowly read out these words which are taken from the Bible:

'God's power is like the rising of the sun: rays flash from him.'

Prayer

Some children may like to conclude the assembly with a short prayer, perhaps written by one of them, about the power of the sun and its significance in their lives.

St Francis of Assisi wrote a beautiful and well-known prayer called 'Brother Sun and Sister Moon' which would also be suitable here. It can be found in many anthologies, including the *Kingfisher Book of Prayers for Children*.

Music

End the gathering with a simple song like 'I Love the Sun', which is available in many school hymn books or choose an appropriate piece from the Resources section in this book.

SIGNS OF SUMMER

This assembly allows children to experience the pleasures of the summer at first hand!

This gathering is planned for a warm, sunny and pleasant day in early summer and should take place in the open air. A garden or outside play area would be suitable locations, but if these are unavailable, the children should be escorted to a nearby park or countryside area.

The gathering is designed to encourage the children to think carefully about the main characteristics of the summer months and to increase their appreciation of the beauty of the natural world.

Introduction

Take the children outside to your chosen area and (with proper supervision) allow them to spend a few quiet moments wandering about, either alone or with a partner within the limits of a set space.

Encourage them to look and listen for signs of summer – bees buzzing, flowers and plants growing, butterflies fluttering and to notice the sunshine and shadows.

After a few moments, invite the children to come and sit in a circle or group on the grass.

What to do

Invite the children to share their thoughts, reflections and experiences with each other.

Ask individual children to present any work which they may have completed about the summer – stories, rhymes and poems could be performed and models, paintings and drawings displayed.

Make appropriate links between the children's thoughts and the work which they have completed and take care to highlight some of the key features of the summer season.

Reflection

Give each child a small, fresh leaf to hold.

Ask the children to look at their leaves in silence, noticing every detail of colour, shape and structure. Encourage them to feel the texture of the leaves by stroking each side gently with the tips of their fingers. Invite them to brush the leaves across their cheeks and to smell their scent.

Prayer

Some children may wish to say a prayer to thank God for the beauty of the natural world, especially in summer time.

In conclusion, offer the children a final opportunity for silent thought and reflection, suggesting that they may wish to close their eyes for a moment.

Music

End the gathering with an extract from 'Summer' from *The Four Seasons* by Vivaldi as the children leave the area.

Collective worship in schools

The assemblies outlined are suitable for use with children in nurseries and playgroups, but would need to be adapted for use with pupils at registered schools. As a result of legislation enacted in 1944, 1988 and 1993, there are now specific points to be observed when developing a programme of Collective Acts of Worship in a school.

Further guidance will be available from your local SACRE – Standing Advisory Council for RE.

THEMES
for early years

POEMS AND ACTION RHYMES

A LETTER TO THE GROWN-UPS

Dear Grown-ups,

Please leave all the flowers there
And don't cut down the trees.
We need the trees to make fresh air
And flowers to feed the bees.

Please don't always use your car
To take you everywhere
Because the fumes go very far
And heat the atmosphere.

Then soon the sun will be too hot
And all the plants will die.
So please get out and walk a lot
To see the clear blue sky.

Then we will run and jump and play
And grow up strong and tall.
Then we'll be happy every day
And we will thank you all.

With love from the children.

Stevie Ann Wilde

SUMMER SKIES

Swallows dip and swoop and dart,
across the summer sky.
They use the air to lift their wings,
and carry them up high.

Balloons will float when full of air,
and kites, when there's a breeze.
All colours and shapes and sizes,
flying above the trees.

White clouds, fluffy clouds,
floating across the sky.
Can you make out different shapes,
as they sail by?

Jan Pollard

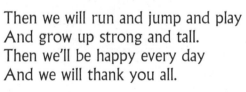

PHOTOCOPIABLE RESOURCES

COVER UP

When it's a lovely sunny day
I ask my mum if I can play.
She says, "You can, but first of all –
Before you go and get your ball –
Please find your floppy old sun-hat,
Your baggy T-shirt after that.
Bring me the sun cream from the drawer
The sun might burn and make you sore."
She makes me cover up always.
Protect *your* skin on summer days!

Wendy Larmont

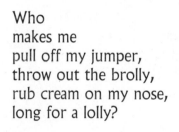

RIDDLE-ME-REE

Who
brings out
the lawnmower,
my T-shirts,
a thousand dandelions?

Who
makes me
pull off my jumper,
throw out the brolly,
rub cream on my nose,
long for a lolly?

Who
makes the cuckoo
cuckoo?

You can feel it, not hear it,
nor touch or go near it!
It's huge, it's hot
there's only one...
Can you guess what it is?
It is
the
....!

Judith Nicholls

SUMMER STORM

There's a rumble in the distance
A grumble in the cloud.
At first it growls quite gently
Then it roars out loud.

There's a hammering of raindrops
A-bouncing fat and bold
The jagged flash of lightning
Cuts the sky with gold.

There's a whispering of anger
Across hills far away.
The clouds so black and heavy
Now are white and grey.

There's a peaceful, fragrant silence.
The wet leaves drip and shine
The summer storm has ended
All is fresh and fine.

Wendy Larmont

SUNSHINE AND SHADOWS

The sun is shining bright today
Look, my shadow's come to play
I move my arm, I shake my shoe,
My shadow does all that I do
Twist and shake and turn about
But when the sun's no longer out
My shadow has to go away
But he'll come back another day.

Elizabeth Dale

SUMMER SENSES

My ears tell me it's summer,
I can hear bees and lawnmowers buzzing.

My eyes tell me it's summer,
I can see blue sky and butterflies.

My nose tells me it's summer,
I can smell sun cream and grass cuttings.

My tongue tells me it's summer,
I can taste barbecued chicken and ice lollies.

My whole body tells me it's summer,
I can role down a grassy hill and land with a
bump!

Val Jeans-Jakobsson

STICKY LICKY

In the summer,
When it's sunny,
Eating ice-cream
Can be funny.

Ice-cream melts
And drips so fast
It's quite hard
To make it last.

It's so lovely,
Sweet and licky,
But when it drips,
You get sticky.

I get ice-cream
On my clothes,
In my hair
And up my nose.

My dad says
I should eat less;
Ice-cream plus me
Equals — mess!

Tony Bradman

WHAT AM I?

I am light as a breeze,
a puff of pink smoke;
a chin-sticker, lip-gripper,
fluffy pink joke!

I cling to your fingers,
I curl round your thumb;
then like a small duvet
I wrap round your tongue.

Judith Nicholls

PHOTOCOPIABLE RESOURCES

STRAWBERRY PIE

Pick a strawberry,
pop a strawberry
on your tongue;
squeeze it hard
and taste the juice...
pick another one!

One for the basket,
two for the mouth,
three for supper,
four for tea;
five for the dish,
then open wide!
Here's the plumpest
and that's for me!

Pick a strawberry,
pop a strawberry
on your tongue;
squeeze it hard
and taste the juice...
now they've GONE!

Judith Nicholls

WATCH THE WHEAT GROW

	Actions
Here is the wheat	Arms up in the air
Growing so tall	
Here is the farmer	Hand above eyes, head turning to look
Watching it all.	around.
Here is the sunshine	
Here is the rain.	Hands spread out in a circle.
Now is the time	Fingers make rain actions.
We can harvest the grain.	Two hands together to make a cutting action.
Here is the miller	
To grind it to flour.	
Here is the baker	Make a large circular action in front.
To bake it one hour.	
	Kneading the dough.
Here are the children	
Waiting to eat	
Sliced bread and butter	The children point to each other then
That's made from the wheat.	pretend to eat a slice of bread and butter.
	Children to end by saying 'Mmmmmm!'

Stevie Ann Wilde

PHOTOCOPIABLE RESOURCES

READY FOR THE BEACH

First we put on swimsuits,
Swimsuits, swimsuits,
Now we're wearing swimsuits
Ready for the beach.

Then we put on flipflops,
Flipflops, flipflops,
Now we're wearing flipflops
Ready for the beach.

Then we put on sun cream...

Then we put on sun-hats...

Then we put on glasses...

(add other verses for other items)

Don't forget the beach towels,
Beach towels, beach towels,
Now we've got our beach towels
We're off to the beach!

Sue Cowling

SEASIDE SONG

(finger rhyme)

Here are the cliffs.

Here are the seas.

Here are the waves.

And here is the breeze.

Here are the fishes
that dart and play.

And here are the seagulls

that fly away.

Tony Mitton

(hold hands upright and together,
palms toward face)

(hold hands horizontal and together, palms
down, fingers pointing away)

(rock hands sideways, outwards and back
to make waves that 'crest')

(make sweeping fluttery movement with one
hand travelling sideways in front of body)

(wiggle fingers of both hands rapidly
while moving hands around in front
of body)

(make seagull by linking thumbs
and fluttering hands for wings)

(fly your gull up and to one side,
then drop one hand down and use
the other to mime looking far away
over eyes)

PHOTOCOPIABLE RESOURCES

OUR SCHOOL FÊTE

At our summer fête
there's a big marquee
full of people selling
cakes and tea.

There are stalls with toys,
books, knitted things.
Games — win a prize
when you throw three rings.

There's a bouncy castle,
a talent show,
knock down the tins
at 10p a throw.

Enter a raffle,
see the prize marrow,
whang your welly,
race a wheelbarrow...

On our school field
in the summer sun
everyone's laughing,
they're having such fun.

Penny Kent

CARNIVAL

Carnival in London
On a lovely August day,
Steel bands play calypsos
As the dancers swing and sway.

"Please jump up and join us",
As the floats move down the street.
Ladies from their kitchens
Bring out spicy food to eat.

Gaily painted bodies,
Flashing jewellery, masks of gold,
Feathers, beads and satins,
Costumes stunning to behold.

Happy people watch
The Caribbean Masquerade,
Singing with the music
In the Carnival Parade.

Wendy Larmont

FIVE WOBBLY JELLY FISH

(Start with children standing in a circle)

	Actions
Five wobbly jelly fish	*5 fingers – wobble body*
Sitting on the sands	*sit down*
Played Ring o' Roses	*hold hands in circle*
By holding out their hands	*show hands*
One wobbly jelly fish	*1 finger – wobble body*
Saw a little boat	*hands above eyes, looking*
And sailed far away	*sailing movement with hand*
On a sandcastle's moat	*draw circle*
Four wobbly jelly fish	*4 fingers – wobble body*
Paddling near the shore	*lift skirt or trousers to paddle*
Played Ring o' Roses	*hold hands in circle*
And shouted out for more.	*cup hands to mouth*
One wobbly jelly fish	*1 finger – wobble body*
Gave a little moan	*hand over mouth*
As he bumped his toe	*hop, rub toe*
On the edge of a stone	*draw round edge of hand*
Three wobbly jelly fish	*3 fingers – wobble body*
Swimming in the sea	*breast stroke action*
Played Ring o' Roses	*hold hands*
Before having tea.	*pretend to eat*
One wobbly jelly fish	*1 finger – wobble body*
Made a little wish	*close eyes, look thoughtful*
And was pulled away	*extend arms clutch own hands*
On the tail of a fish	*wavy movement with hand*
Two wobbly jelly fish	*2 fingers – wobble body*
Climbing on a rock	*climbing movement*
Played Ring o' Roses	*hold hands*
Then they had a shock.	*mouth open, hands held up*
One wobbly jelly fish	*1 finger – wobble body*
Went too near the edge	*teeter on toes*
Fell off the rock	*fall down*
And landed on a ledge	*sit up*
One wobbly jelly fish	*1 finger – wobble body*
Playing all alone	*turn around*
Played Ring o' Roses	*hold own hands in circle*
And then went home!	*walking action, wave*
	goodbye

Brenda Williams

STORIES

STRAWBERRY AND CREAM

"Sarah," called Mum, "Do you want to go shopping?"

Sarah jumped off her bed.

"Can I push the trolley?"

"If you're careful," Mum said. "It's hot again. Bring your sun-hat." She smiled at Sarah round the bedroom door. "Shall we take that birthday money Gran gave you?"

"Yes please."

Downstairs Sarah helped to write the shopping list. Her writing didn't always go where she wanted, and she didn't know all the sounds yet. She wrote B for bread, M for milk and J for jam. Mum wrote the other bits.

Mum drove carefully, with Sarah strapped in the safety seat in the back. On the way to town she saw a big board against a gate.

"P...I...C..." She tried to read the words chalked on the board.

"Good girl, yes" said Mum. "Pick. Pick your own."

Sarah smiled. "What does it mean?"

Mum explained. "People can go in that field to pick strawberries."

"Do you have to pay money?"

"Oh yes," laughed Mum, "but not as much as at the shops."

At the supermarket Mum gave Sarah a one pound coin. She put it carefully in the slot in a trolley to free it, and they went inside. While Mum chose packets and tins Sarah pushed the trolley carefully. Soon the trolley got too heavy for Sarah, so Mum pushed instead.

When they got to the toys Sarah saw some lovely teddies, pink ones, yellow, and blue.

"That's what I want to buy with Gran's money," she said.

"All right," said Mum.

"I love this pink teddy, and he wants to come and live with us." Sarah hugged him.

In the car on the way home Mum asked "What's teddy's name?"

"I don't know yet," Sarah said.

At the Pick Your Own, Mum slowed down and drove into the field.

"How about some strawberries for lunch?" She looked at Sarah.

"YES, PLEASE."

PHOTOCOPIABLE RESOURCES

There were lots of people in the field. Mum parked, then they locked up, got out, and went to a lady wearing an apron. She gave Mum and Sarah some baskets and told them where to start picking. Soon Sarah learnt to find the best strawberries.

They filled four baskets. Then they took them to the lady in the apron. She weighed them, and Mum paid the lady for the strawberries. At home Sarah helped to put away the shopping. For lunch they had boiled egg and toast soldiers. Dad turned his eggshell upside down and drew a face on it. Sarah laughed. They had strawberries and cream next.

"Now I'm four," said Sarah, "I like strawberries best."

Mum smiled. "I expect you'll like home-made strawberry jam too. I'm going to make some soon."

Making jam was interesting. Sarah helped to wash and weigh the fruit, then boil it in a pan with lots of sugar. There was a lot of stirring to do.

Soon there were ten pots of warm red jam on the kitchen table.

Dad looked at them "Mmmmm," he said, "Is that all for us?"

"Well, there's a pot for Gran," said Mum.

Sarah suddenly remembered.

"Gran! My birthday money... Where's my teddy!"

"Yes. Where is he?" Mum asked.

Sarah began to cry. "I don't know."

Mum sat down and hugged her. "We'll find him. Don't worry."

They looked in the cupboard in case Teddy had been put away with the cornflakes. But there was no Teddy. They looked in the car. Still no Teddy. Then Sarah remembered.

"I took him to pick strawberries. He's in the field."

"Right," said Dad, "Come on. I expect he's sitting waiting for you."

Dad drove to the field. The gate was tied up. Everyone had gone. They couldn't see a pink teddy anywhere. Sarah tried hard not to cry.

Dad said "We'll go to the supermarket and buy another. They don't shut until 8 o'clock tonight."

In the supermarket the pink teddies had been sold. Sarah chose a yellow one but what she really wanted was the lost pink one.

At bedtime, Sarah hugged the new teddy but she couldn't forget the pink one. What if it rained? Would he be frightened there, alone in the dark? Or perhaps another little boy or girl had found Teddy and taken him home. "I expect they will look after him and love him just like me," she thought, and she went to sleep.

Straight after breakfast Sarah went with Dad and Mum to the Pick Your Own. The lady with the apron smiled at them.

"Hello," she said, "Here again."

Mum told her about the lost teddy.

"Well, nobody handed in a teddy, but you can have a look for yourselves," she said. Sarah ran along the rows of strawberry plants. Mum and Dad walked slowly, looking this way and that. Sarah remembered sitting Teddy near the hedge so that he would be in the shade. All at once she saw him: a patch of pink that was definitely not a strawberry! He had fallen forward onto his nose. She called to Mum and Dad, and picked him up. After a big hug and a bit of a brush down, he looked much better.

Back home Sarah took pink teddy up to meet yellow teddy. They sat side by side on her bed. They were already good friends.

"Now I know your names," she said. She patted pink teddy. "Your name is Strawberry." Then she patted yellow teddy. "Your name is Cream. Strawberry and Cream!"

Sue Croft

PHOTOCOPIABLE RESOURCES

DISAPPEARING PUDDLES

"It's hot again," said Sam to his little brother Tom, as he looked out of the bedroom window.

It had been a long, hot summer. Every day the two boys had played in the garden wearing only shorts, a T-shirt and big hats.

"It's always hot." said Tom standing on tiptoe to peep through the window.

"Look," said Sam, "the birds are already thirsty, they are drinking water from the bird bath."

Tom watched for a while, and then he said, "I'm thirsty too," and he ran off downstairs to breakfast.

A little later that day, when they were playing on their slide, Tom noticed that the bird bath was empty.

"The birds have drunk all that water," he said to Sam.

Sam looked, and sure enough, the bird bath was empty.

"I know," he said, "let's get out our watering cans and fill it up again."

They had great fun, climbing up to the kitchen sink for water and running backwards and forwards to fill the bird bath. Even Flop, their little dog joined in the game, racing and skidding along beside them.

"What a mess you're making!" said Mummy crossly, as they dripped splashes across the kitchen floor.

"It's for the birds," shouted Tom. It's an emergency, they need more water!"

Soon the bird bath was full to the brim, and there were large puddles on the path where it had slopped over. Flop had run so hard, she stopped to have a drink from the puddles.

Later, when Mummy called them in for tea, they saw that the bath was almost empty again.

"The birds have drunk it all again," said Sam. "And Flop has drunk up all the puddles."

"They must have been very, very thirsty," thought Tom as he went inside.

The next day was washing day, and Mummy put the wet clothes on the line. Tom and Sam had their paddling pool out, and they splashed and paddled till snack time.

"Your hair's soaking wet," said Sam as he saw the water trickling down Tom's face.

"So is yours," Tom laughed, as he shook his head to make the water fly off.

But by lunch time, their hair and the washing were dry. So was the bird bath.

"Where does the water go?" asked Tom. "The birds can't drink off my hair!"

"I'm going to ask Dad tonight," said Sam puzzled. And he did.

The next day, when Tom was filling the bird bath again, Sam told him, "Daddy says the sun drinks it."

"How?" asked Tom.

"I don't know how, but he does. Dad says so."

"The sun must have a very long drinking straw!" said Tom trying to work out how the sun could reach the bird bath. They both laughed and ran off to play.

During the afternoon, a sudden sharp thunderstorm blew up, and they had a very quick shower of rain.

Just as the rain stopped, Daddy arrived home. His car was wet from the rain, but as the sun came out, steam started to rise from the warm bonnet.

"Your car's on fire Daddy," shouted Tom.

Daddy smiled and said, "No, it's just the sun turning the water into steam."

"So that's how the sun drinks the bird bath!" exclaimed Tom.

"It's called evaporation." said Daddy.

Brenda Williams

HARRY'S SEASIDE HOLIDAY

Harry was really excited because today they were going on holiday to the seaside. He'd never been to the seaside but he'd seen pictures of it and he couldn't wait to get there!

It was a long journey. "Are we nearly there?" Harry asked for the umpteenth time.

"Just a little longer," Mum told him. She'd been saying that for over an hour. Harry sighed and put another story tape in his cassette player.

"Here we are!" Dad said at last, turning into a huge caravan park. Their caravan was on the end. It was very big and Harry had a little bedroom all to himself.

Early the next morning, Harry was woken up by squawking and something pattering on the roof. For a moment he wondered what it was, then he remembered he was on holiday.

"Can you hear the seagulls?" Dad asked, poking his head around the door. "Aren't they noisy?"

Harry grinned and jumped out of bed. "Are we going to the beach?" he asked.

"Later on, when we've had breakfast," Dad told him.

Harry took his bucket and spade to the beach. He ran eagerly across the soft sand. Then he stopped and stared. Right in front of him was the sea. It was the scariest thing he'd ever seen. Masses and masses of water that went on forever and ever. Huge waves rolled out of it and splashed on to the sand. Harry was terrified.

"Fancy a paddle?" asked Dad.

Harry shook his head. "I'm not going in there!" he said, his voice quivering.

"There's no need to be scared. I'll hold your hand." said Mum. Harry shook his head.

"Look at all the other children playing in the sea," said Dad. "They're having lots of fun!"

Harry shook his head again. "No!" he said firmly.

So Harry played in the sand instead. But every now and again he sneaked a look over at the children playing in the sea and wished he was brave enough to join them.

The next day they went down to the beach again. "We're going to have a paddle in the sea," said Mum. "Are you coming Harry?"

Harry shook his head. "I'll play in the sand instead," he said.

Harry watched as Mum and Dad paddled in the sea, splashing each other and laughing.

"Come and join us, Harry!" they called. But Harry wouldn't.

After a while, Mum and Dad came out of the sea. "Let's build a sandcastle now," said Dad. "We'll build the biggest sandcastle in the world."

"Yeah!" grinned Harry, cheering up.

They built a really big sandcastle and Mum gave Harry a flag to stick on the top.

"Now we need some water for the moat," said Dad. "We'll go and get some from the sea."

"I'm not," said Harry.

"We need lots of water, so you'll have to help carry it," said Dad.

So Harry held Dad's hand tight and they walked right to the edge of the sea. Harry tried to keep his feet out of the water as he filled up his bucket but a wave gently lapped over them. It was lovely and cool.

They carefully carried the water back to the sandcastle and poured it into the moat. Then they went to fetch some more. This time Harry stepped a little nearer to the sea. He bent down, dipped his hand in the water and splashed it around. The sea didn't seem so scary now.

"Shall we have a little paddle?" asked Dad.

"Okay," said Harry. He and Dad paddled in the sea. Then a wave came rolling towards them. "Let's jump it!" said Dad, holding Harry's hand. They both jumped as the wave came towards them. Harry giggled as it splashed over them.

"I like the sea now," he said. "It's brilliant!"

And he ran off to jump another wave.

Karen King

MR RABBIT AND THE MOON

Mr Rabbit went down the road. He saw a pool of water.

"I will look in the water," said Mr Rabbit. "I will see if I look good."

Mr Rabbit looked in the water. He did look good but the moon was in the water.

"The moon is in the water," said Mr Rabbit. "Come and look, Mrs Mole." Mrs Mole looked in the water.

"The moon is in the water," said Mrs Mole. "Come and look, Mr Rat." Mr Rat looked in the water.

"The moon is in the water," said Mr Rat. "Come and look, Mrs Owl." Mrs Owl looked in the water.

"Look up," said Mrs Owl. "The moon is not in the water."

Mr Rabbit, Mrs Mole and Mr Rat looked up. The moon was in the sky. "We are silly," they said.

SONGS

POT-POURRI

Pick Sum - mer flow'rs with the sweet - est smell, Keep those pe - tals and dry them well.

When the Win - ter's dark and grey, The scent of those pet - als will cheer the day.

Sue Nicholls

PLAYING OUT

Bounce a ball, skip and run, Play - ing out is such fun. Hop - scotch, hide and seek,

Play - ing out is such fun. When my friends come round to play, We have such a

love - ly day. Play - ing out be - neath the sun, Play - ing out is such fun.

Johanne Levy

PHOTOCOPIABLE RESOURCES

IN THE SKY

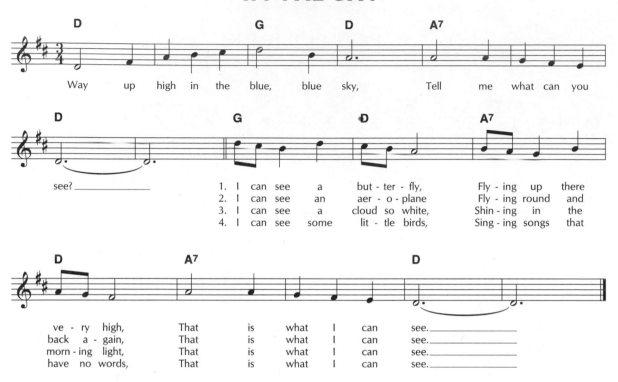

Way up high in the blue, blue sky, Tell me what can you see?

1. I can see a but-ter-fly, Fly-ing up there ve-ry high, That is what I can see.
2. I can see an aer-o-plane Fly-ing round and back a-gain, That is what I can see.
3. I can see a cloud so white, Shin-ing in the morn-ing light, That is what I can see.
4. I can see some lit-tle birds, Sing-ing songs that have no words, That is what I can see.

Barbara Moore

IN THE HEAT

Chorus

Keep cool in the hot sun, Keep cool and you'll have more fun, Co-ver up with all you've got, Sun on your skin is just too hot!

Verse

Put on your glas-ses, put on your hat. Stay in the shade if you fan-cy that. Pro-tect your-self from the burn-ing sun, and you can en-joy your-self all day long.

D.C. al Fine

Vikki MacRae

SUN AND SAND

1. Sing a song of Sum - mer, A pock - et full of sand,

Sing a song of Sum - mer, An ice - cream in my hand.

Sing a song of summer
A pocket full of shells.
Sing a song of summer
And sniff the summer smells.

Sing a song of summer
A pocket full of rhymes.
Sing a song of summer
I love the summer time.

Words: Trevor Millum

Music: Gill Parker, based on Sing a Song of Sixpence (Traditional)

SUMMER STREET PARTY

1. Let's have a par - ty, Let's have a par - ty, Let's have a par - ty, a par - ty in the street.
2. Let's find a part - ner, Let's find a part - ner, Let's find a part - ner, a part - ner in the street.
3. Let's make a four - some, Let's make a four - some, Let's make a four - some, a four - some in the street.
4. Let's make a cir - cle, Let's make a cir - cle, Let's make a cir - cle, a cir - cle in the street.

Clap, clap, roll your hands, Clap, clap, roll your hands, Clap, clap, roll your hands and stamp your feet.

Actions

1. All children in space of their own, do actions as written.

2. Children get into pairs then do actions facing partner.

3. Children get into fours then do actions in small circle.

4. Children make class circle then do actions.

Ann Bryant

PACK MY SUITCASE

Pack my suit-case, Pack my suit-case, Find my ted-dy, Find my ted-dy, Wave to Gran-dad, Wave to Gran-dad,

Sit-ting in a train, Sit-ting in a train, Go-ing on a hol-i - day, Go-ing on a hol-i - day.

This is an echo song where the children echo each line after you have sung it to them. When the children are familiar with the song, one of them could be the leader. Repeat the song a few times, going on different transport each time, for instance: Sitting in a coach, Sitting in a plane, and so on.

You can change Find my teddy, to Find my sun-hat, and so on. Let the children suggest their own ideas.

You could also play a game where you tap the rhythm of the words Pack my suitcase or Sitting in a train. Can the children identify which word-rhythm you were tapping?

Susan Eames

BY THE SEA

1. This is the way we jump the waves, jump the waves, jump the waves.

This is the way we jump the waves, When we're by the sea.

2. This is the way we build a castle.
3. This is the way we dig a hole.
4. This is the way we eat ice-cream.
5. This is the way we ride a donkey.

Words: Barbara Moore

Tune – Here we go round the Mulberry Bush (Traditional)

PHOTOCOPIABLE ACTIVITIES

THEMES
for early years

Name_____

In the mirror

Can you colour in the pictures which are reflections?
Now draw one of your own.

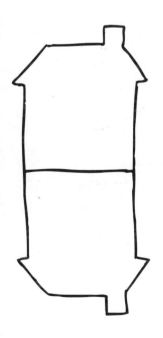

THEMES
for early years

Name_____

Will it melt?

Which of these things change in the heat of the sun?
Can you colour them in?

THEMES
for early years

In the desert

Colour in all the things you might find in the desert.

Name _____

THEMES
for early years

Name _____

Crossing the road

How do you cross the road? Put these pictures in the right order.

PHOTOCOPIABLE ACTIVITIES

THEMES
for early years

Name_____

Find the strawberries

How many strawberries can you find?
Colour them red.

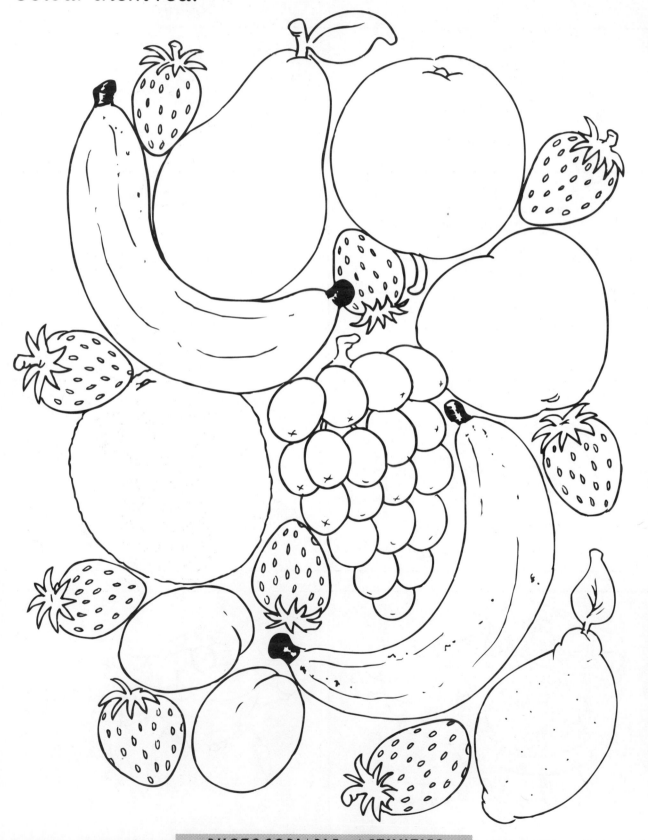

THEMES
for early years

Name_____

Ready to swim

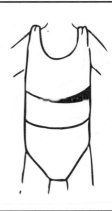

THEMES *for early years*

Dressing up

THEMES
for early years

Name_____

Underwater

Can you help the fish find its way home?

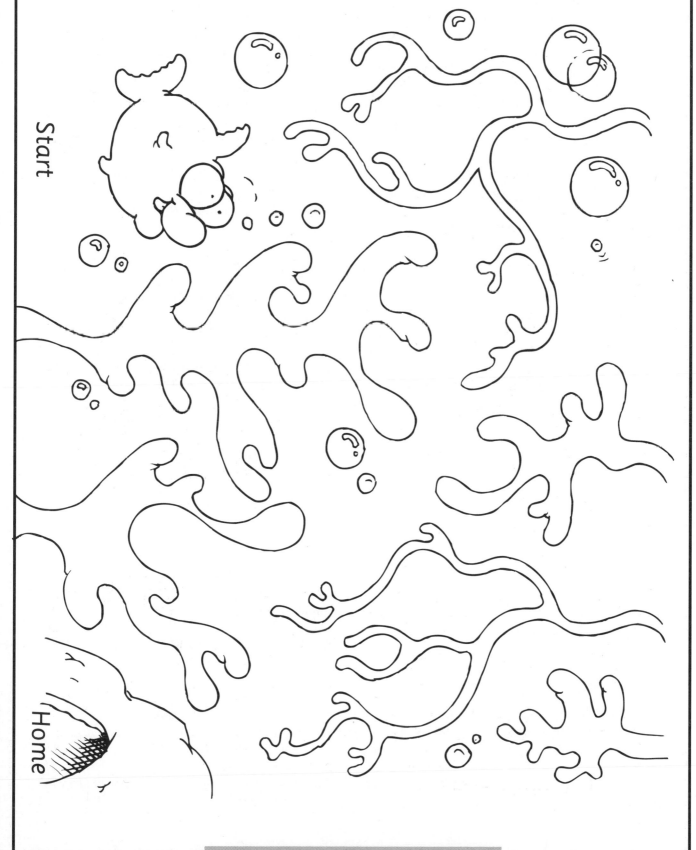

Start

Home

RECOMMENDED MATERIALS

INFORMATION BOOKS

Cotton from seed to cloth R Riquier (Moonlight Publishing)

Children Just Like Me Susan Elizabeth Copsley (Dorling Kindersley)

'The Bee' *First Discovery* series Ute Fuhr and Raoul Sautai (Moonlight Publishing)

'My Shadow' *Simple Science* series Sheila Gore (A & C Black)

'Victorians' *People in Costume* series Jennifer Ruby (Batsford)

'The Planets' and 'The Sun and the Moon' *Starry Sky* series Patrick Moore (Riverswift)

What is the Sun? Reeve Lindbergh (Walker Books)

'Sun and Us' *Weather* series Jillian Powell (Belitha Press)

'What makes a flower grow?' *Starting Point Science* series Susan Mayes (Usbourne)

'Deserts' *Wonders of the Earth* series Neil Morris (Crabtree Publishing Compnay)

'Ice-cream' *Favourite Food* series Brian Moses and Mike Gordon (Wayland)

'Fruit' *Threads* series Miriam Moss (A & C Black)

'Fruit' *All About Food* series Cecilia Fitzsimons (Zoe Books Ltd)

'A Victorian Kitchen' *Living in History* series Peter Chrisp (Heinemann)

Transport then and now Helena Ramsay (Evans Bros)

'Journeys' *History from Photographs* series Kathleen Cox and Pat Hughes (Wayland)

TEACHERS' BOOKS

Stonehenge: A Teacher's Handbook Carol Andersson (English Heritage)

Costume Since 1945 Dierdre Clancy (Herbert Press)

'Festivals and Celebrations' *Bright Ideas for Early Years* series Rhona Whiteford and Jim Fitzsimmons (Scholastic)

STORY BOOKS

Kofi and the Butterflies Sandra Horn (Tamarind Books)

The Very Busy Spider Eric Carle (Hamish Hamilton)

Ladybird Moves Home Richard Fowler (Doubleday)

Sports Day! Nick Butterworth and Mick Inkpen (Hodder)

'Sandcastle' *Little Kippers* series Mick Inkpen (Hodder)

'At the Park' and 'Carnival' *Oxford Reading Tree* series Roderick Hunt (Oxford University Press)

One Summer Day Kim Lewis (Walker Books)

Carnival Robin Ballard (W Morrow)

Spot at the Carnival Eric Hill (Warne)

Magical Bicycle Berlie Doherty (Picture Lions)

My Cat Jack Patricia Casey (Walker Books)

'Strawberry Jam' and 'The Barbecue' *Oxford Reading Tree* series (Oxford University Press)

Gregory Cool Caroline Binch (Frances Lincoln)

Grandpa on Holiday Rob Lewis (Red Fox)

Lucy and Tom at the Seaside Shirley Hughes (Picture Puffin)

Boo and Baa at Sea Olof and Lena Landstrom (Raben and Sjogren)

Sail Away Donald Crews (W Morrow)

POETRY

Witch's Brew: And Other Poems Wes Magee (Cambridge University Press)

'Poetry' *Scholastic Collections* compiled by Wes Magee (Scholastic)

MUSIC

Use recordings of these pieces of music to enhance your work with the children.

Flight of the Bumblebee Rimsky Korsakov

The Planets Gustav Holst

The Seasons Vivaldi

Beethoven's Pastoral Symphony

Haydn's Creation

Scherazade Rimsky-Korsakov

A Sea Symphony Vaughan Williams

ART

Look in art books for reproductions of these famous paintings to show the children, in order to stimulate their 'summer' work.

The Fighting Téméraire WJM Turner

Twelve Sunflowers in a Vase Vincent Van Gogh

The Seine at Asnières Auguste Renoir

Yachts LS Lowry

Entrance to a Harbour LS Lowry

San Giorgio Maggiore: sunset, The Red Boats, Argenteuil, Terrace at Sainte–Adresse, Soleil Levant, The River, Impression Sunrise, Summer, The Meadow, The Promenade, Woman with a Parasol, Vetheuil Church all by Claude Monet